CHECK-LIST OF
THE BIRDS OF KANSAS

CHECK-LIST OF THE BIRDS OF KANSAS

HARRISON BRUCE TORDOFF,
E. RAYMOND HALL,
A. BYRON LEONARD,
ROBERT W. WILSON

ISBN: 978-93-5614-187-2

Published: 1956

© 2022
LECTOR HOUSE LLP

LECTOR HOUSE LLP
E-MAIL: lectorpublishing@gmail.com

UNIVERSITY OF KANSAS PUBLICATIONS
MUSEUM OF NATURAL HISTORY

EDITORS: E. RAYMOND HALL, CHAIRMAN, A. BYRON LEONARD,
ROBERT W. WILSON

Volume 8, No. 5, pp. 307-359, 1 figure in text

March 10, 1956

CHECK-LIST OF
THE BIRDS OF KANSAS

BY

HARRISON B. TORDOFF

1956

CHECK-LIST OF THE BIRDS OF KANSAS

Kansas was one of the first states for which a detailed book on birds was published (N. S. Goss, "History of the Birds of Kansas," Topeka, Kansas, 1891). Ornithological progress in Kansas in recent years, however, has not kept pace with work in many other states. As a result, knowledge of the birds of Kansas today is not sufficiently detailed to make possible a modern, definitive report. One purpose of this check-list is to show gaps in our information on birds of the state. Each student of birds can contribute importantly by keeping accurate records of nesting, distribution, and migration of any species in Kansas and by making these records available through publication in appropriate journals. The Museum of Natural History at the University of Kansas solicits records and specimens which contribute to our knowledge of birds in Kansas. Files and collections at the Museum are available to any qualified person for study.

The last state-wide list of birds was prepared by W. S. Long (Trans. Kansas Acad. Sci., 43, 1940:433-456). This list and the unpublished thesis from which the list was abstracted have been of great value in preparing the present report. Many other persons have contributed and among these the names of the following must be mentioned because of the value of their contributions: Ivan L. Boyd, L. B. Carson, Arthur L. Goodrich, Jr., Richard Graber, Jean Graber, Harold C. Hedges, R. F. Miller, John M. Porter, and Marvin D. Schwilling.

Full standing in this check-list has been given only to species for which at least one specimen from Kansas has been examined by some qualified student. Exceptions to this admittedly arbitrary rule have been made in three cases, Trumpeter Swan, Turkey, and Carolina Paroquet, because there is no reason to doubt that each of these three species once occurred in Kansas and because opportunity for obtaining specimens from Kansas has been lost through disappearance of the species from the state. Other species reported from the state but not authenticated by specimens have been relegated to the Hypothetical List and their names and my remarks concerning these birds are enclosed in brackets. This procedure is intended to encourage collection of such species; it is not intended necessarily to indicate doubt of a record. In the case of a carefully identified but uncollected accidental, opportunity for obtaining a specimen may not exist again for a long period. This is unfortunate but emphasizes the need for judicious collecting.

A total of 375 species (or 459 species and subspecies), of which four are introduced, is included in this check-list. Additionally, 15 species are discussed in the Hypothetical List. An asterisk (*) preceding an account indicates positive evidence of breeding in Kansas of the species so marked. The total of species known to have bred at least once in the state is 173. Nomenclature in this list follows the American Ornithologists' Union "Check-List of North American Birds" (1931, 4th edition) and its supplements. Species on the Hypothetical List are included in their current taxonomic position in the main list.

Gavia immer (Brünnich). Common Loon. Uncommon transient throughout state.

No subspecies recognized.

Gavia stellata (Pontoppidan). Red-throated Loon. Rare transient. One specimen: female (Univ. Michigan Mus. Zool. 65778), Marais des Cygnes River, near Ottawa, Franklin County, October 20, 1925, Captain Joe R. White. Several sight records from Shawnee and Johnson counties within past 10 years.

No subspecies recognized.

Colymbus grisegena. Red-necked Grebe. Rare transient. One specimen: female (KU 7697), Kansas River east of Lawrence, Douglas County, October 29, 1910, Logan I. Evans.

Subspecies in Kansas: *C. g. holböllii* (Reinhardt).

Colymbus auritus. Horned Grebe. Rare transient. Two authentic specimens: Manhattan, Riley County, September 30, 1878; male (KU 27465), 2½ miles north of Lawrence, Douglas County, November 16, 1945, E. C. Olson and Ralph L. Montell. Several sight records, from eastern, central, and western Kansas.

Subspecies in Kansas: *C. a. cornutus* Gmelin.

Colymbus caspicus. Eared Grebe. Regular transient throughout state; more common than Horned Grebe.

Subspecies in Kansas: *C. c. californicus* (Heermann).

Aechmophorus occidentalis (Lawrence). Western Grebe. Rare transient, perhaps more common in west but status poorly known.

No subspecies recognized.

* *Podilymbus podiceps*. Pied-billed Grebe. Common transient and irregular summer resident, rare winter resident.

Subspecies in Kansas: *P. p. podiceps* (Linnaeus).

Pelecanus erythrorhynchos Gmelin. White Pelican. Common transient throughout state. Occasional individuals, probably sick or wounded, remain beyond normal migration periods in spring and fall.

No subspecies recognized.

Pelecanus occidentalis. Brown Pelican. Accidental. One specimen: adult, sex not determined (KU 10468), Parker, Linn County, June, 1916, found dead by G. G. McConnell. One seen at Wichita, Sedgwick County, by R. H. Sullivan, April 25, 1910.

Subspecies in Kansas: *P. o. carolinensis* Gmelin.

* *Phalacrocorax auritus*. Double-crested Cormorant. Regular transient, in small

to moderate numbers. One nesting record: several nests, eggs, and small young seen, Cheyenne Bottoms, Barton County, August, 1951, Otto Tiemeier.

Subspecies in Kansas: *P. a. auritus* (Lesson).

Phalacrocorax olivaceus. Mexican Cormorant. Accidental. One record: specimen taken 4 miles south of Lawrence, Douglas County, April 2, 1872. Present location unknown but specimen identified by S. F. Baird and R. Ridgway.

Subspecies in Kansas: *P. o. mexicanus* (Brandt).

Anhinga anhinga. Water-turkey. Accidental. Several specimens and sight observations are on record but most are prior to 1900. Several records and one specimen at Cheyenne Bottoms, Barton County, since 1928 (Frank Robl). In recent years, some reported Water-turkeys have proved to be cormorants.

Subspecies in Kansas: *A. a. leucogaster* (Vieillot).

Fregata magnificens. Man-o'-war-bird. Accidental. One record: specimen (present location unknown) taken on the North Fork of the Solomon River, Osborne County, August 16, 1880, by Frank Lewis.

Subspecies in Kansas: *F. m. rothschildi* Mathews.

* *Ardea herodias.* Great Blue Heron. Common transient and summer resident nesting in widely scattered colonies.

Subspecies in Kansas: three reported, *A. h. herodias* Linnaeus in northeast, *A. h. wardi* Ridgway in southeast, and *A. h. treganzai* Court in west, but status of these poorly known because of lack of sufficient breeding specimens.

Casmerodius albus. American Egret. Regular postbreeding summer visitant; occasional spring and summer resident. No definite nesting record.

Subspecies in Kansas: *C. a. egretta* (Gmelin).

* *Leucophoyx thula.* Snowy Egret. Regular postbreeding summer visitant; rare and local summer resident; occasional in spring. One nesting record: two nests found, summer, 1952, 6 miles north and 4½ miles west of Garden City, Finney County, Marvin D. Schwilling.

Subspecies in Kansas: *L. t. thula* (Molina).

Hydranassa tricolor. Louisiana Heron. Accidental. Two records: specimen taken at Lake Inman, McPherson County, August 9, 1934, by R. E. Mohler and Richard H. Schmidt; one seen, 1½ miles south of Iatan Marsh, Atchison County (near Iatan, Missouri), September 12, 1948, first reported by R. F. Miller and Mr. and Mrs. Ivan L. Boyd, seen by several other observers.

Subspecies in Kansas: *H. t. ruficollis* (Gosse).

* *Florida caerulea.* Little Blue Heron. Regular postbreeding summer visitant; rare and local summer resident; occasional in spring. Usually more common than Snowy Egret. One nesting record: one nest found, summer, 1952, 6 miles north and 4½ miles west of Garden City, Finney County, Marvin D. Schwilling.

Subspecies in Kansas: *F. c. caerulea* (Linnaeus).

* *Butorides virescens.* Green Heron. Common transient and summer resident.

Subspecies in Kansas: *B. v. virescens* (Linnaeus).

* *Nycticorax nycticorax.* Black-crowned Night Heron. Transient and summer resident, breeding in scattered colonies.

Subspecies in Kansas: *N. n. hoactli* (Gmelin).

* *Nyctanassa violacea.* Yellow-crowned Night Heron. Summer resident throughout state, rare in north; numbers perhaps augmented in late summer by postbreeding stragglers.

Subspecies in Kansas: *N. v. violacea* (Linnaeus).

* *Botaurus lentiginosus* (Rackett). American Bittern. Common transient; summer resident locally. Two definite nesting records: nest with 4 newly hatched young (male collected, KU 30468), ½ mile east and 2 miles south of Welda, Anderson County, June 9, 1951, Maurice F. Baker; nest with eggs, 6 miles north and 3½ miles west of Kalvesta, Finney County, summer, 1952, Raymond Erkic (*fide* Marvin D. Schwilling).

No subspecies recognized.

* *Ixobrychus exilis.* Least Bittern. Transient and irregular summer resident. Two nests found at Lake Quivira, Johnson County, June 3, 1949, Harold C. Hedges; on June 28, one of the nests contained 4 eggs, on July 10 this nest was empty. No other definite nesting records.

Subspecies in Kansas: *I. e. exilis* (Gmelin).

Mycteria americana Linnaeus. Wood Ibis. Accidental. Several sight records and one specimen: male (KU 9489), 5 miles north-*east of Goodland, Sherman County, October 4, 1913, Willis Feaster.

No subspecies recognized.

* *Plegadis mexicana* (Gmelin). White-faced Glossy Ibis. Irregular transient and summer visitant; more common in west. One definite nesting record: photograph of downy young ("Kansas Fish and Game," vol. 9, no. 3, Jan. 1952, p. 7) taken at Cheyenne Bottoms, Barton County, presumably in summer of 1951, by L. O. Nossaman. Frank Robl has seen individuals in summer in Cheyenne Bottoms on many occasions. Reports of Eastern Glossy Ibis (*Plegadis falcinellus*) in Kansas probably are based on dark-faced immatures of the present species, although the eastern species has been taken in Oklahoma.

No subspecies recognized.

Ajaia ajaja (Linnaeus). Roseate Spoonbill. Accidental. One authentic specimen (present location not known): male, near Douglass, on Four-Mile Creek, Butler County, March 20, 1899, taken by Dr. R. Matthews, identification verified by Jerold Volk and Wilfred Goodman.

No subspecies recognized.

Phoenicopterus ruber Linnaeus. Flamingo. Accidental. Two birds seen in autumn, 1928, at Little Salt Marsh, Stafford County, one of which was killed on opening day of duck season and now (1955) is mounted at Kansas Forestry, Fish, and Game Commission headquarters at Pratt.

No subspecies recognized.

Olor columbianus (Ord). Whistling Swan. Transient and winter resident, formerly common, now rare. Many specimens are on record; at least four were taken in winter.

No subspecies recognized.

Olor buccinator (Richardson). Trumpeter Swan. Formerly occasional migrant, no longer occurs in Kansas. All specimens from Kansas alleged to be of this species are actually Whistling Swans. The early sight records seem valid, however, and the species should remain on the state list.

No subspecies recognized.

* *Branta canadensis*. Canada Goose. Common transient; some winter in suitable places. This species was found nesting along the Missouri River near Atchison by early explorers. Modern breeding records probably pertain to captives or their descendants.

Subspecies in Kansas: *B. c. moffitti* Aldrich, *B. c. leucopareia* (Brandt), *B. c. minima* Ridgway, and *B. c. hutchinsi* (Richardson) have been collected in Kansas. Additionally, subspecies *interior* Todd and *parvipes* (Cassin) probably pass through the state but no specimens have been saved. Canada Geese of widely varying size are regularly seen in migration.

Branta bernicla. Brant. Accidental. Several sight records and one specimen: unsexed bird (KU 7490), Leavenworth County, November 15, 1879, A. Lange. Some hunters refer to immature Blue Geese as "brant." Orville O. Rice saw 4 brant 2 miles north of Burlington, near the Neosho River, Coffey County, March 24, 1955, that appeared to be Black Brant, *Branta nigricans* (Lawrence).

Subspecies in Kansas: *B. b. hrota* (Müller).

Anser albifrons. White-fronted Goose. Regular transient throughout state, more common in central and western parts.

Subspecies in Kansas: *A. a. frontalis* Baird.

Chen hyperborea. Snow Goose. Common transient throughout state.

Subspecies in Kansas: *C. h. hyperborea* (Pallas).

Chen caerulescens (Linnaeus). Blue Goose. Common transient in east, less common in central and western parts of state. In east, this species predominates in early spring migration whereas the Snow Goose is most numerous later. Hybrids between the two are regularly seen.

No subspecies recognized.

[*Chen rossii* (Cassin). Ross Goose. One reported at Wyandotte County Lake, November 22, 1951, by John Bishop. Placed in Hypothetical List in absence of a specimen.]

Dendrocygna bicolor. Fulvous Tree-duck. Accidental. Frank Robl carefully examined and identified three specimens killed in 1929 or 1930, in Cheyenne Bottoms, Barton County. None saved. Specimens collected also in nearby areas of Missouri.

Subspecies in Kansas: *D. b. helva* Wetmore and Peters, on geographical grounds.

* *Anas platyrhynchos.* Mallard. Abundant transient, regular winter resident, irregular and local summer resident. Modern breeding distribution poorly known but several nests found in widely scattered areas in past years. Nests regularly in Kearny, Finney, and Barton counties.

Subspecies in Kansas: *A. p. platyrhynchos* Linnaeus.

Anas rubripes Brewster. Black Duck. Regular but rare or uncommon transient and winter resident in east and central (Cheyenne Bottoms, Barton County) sections.

No subspecies recognized.

Anas fulvigula. Mottled Duck. Accidental. Four specimens allegedly of this species have been reported. Of these, two are actually Mallards, one is a Gadwall, and one, female, Neosho Falls, Woodson County, March 11, 1876, Goss, is a Mottled Duck.

Subspecies in Kansas: *A. f. maculosa* Sennett.

Anas strepera Linnaeus. Gadwall. Transient and occasional winter resident throughout state. Rare summer resident but no satisfactory nesting record reported.

No subspecies recognized.

* *Anas acuta* Linnaeus. Pintail. Abundant transient throughout state, irregular winter resident, local summer resident nesting in recent years in Barton, Finney, Meade, and Leavenworth counties, but summer distribution poorly known.

No subspecies recognized.

Anas carolinensis Gmelin. Green-winged Teal. Common transient, rare winter resident (records from Meade County and Kansas City).

No subspecies recognized.

* *Anas discors* Linnaeus. Blue-winged Teal. Common transient, locally common summer resident.

No subspecies recognized.

· *Anas cyanoptera.* Cinnamon Teal. Rare transient in east, uncommon or fairly common transient in west.

Subspecies in Kansas: *A. c. septentrionalis* Snyder and Lumsden.

* *Spatula clypeata* (Linnaeus). Shoveller. Common transient throughout state. Frank Robl found a female with young in Cheyenne Bottoms, Barton County, in

approximately 1930. Nest with eggs found 1½ miles south of Friend, Finney County, in spring, 1952, Marvin D. Schwilling.

No subspecies recognized.

[*Mareca penelope* (Linnaeus). European Widgeon. Carl and David Holmes reported a pair at Lake Shawnee, Shawnee County, April 16, 1954. Placed on Hypothetical List until a specimen is taken.]

Mareca americana (Gmelin). Baldpate. Common transient throughout state, rare winter resident.

No subspecies recognized.

* *Aix sponsa* (Linnaeus). Wood Duck. Transient, rare in west to locally common in extreme east. Summer resident in eastern part of state; breeding distribution poorly known.

No subspecies recognized.

* *Aythya americana* (Eyton). Redhead. Fairly common transient and occasional winter resident throughout state. Frank Robl found a nesting pair in Cheyenne Bottoms, Barton County, in 1928 (approximate). The adults were neither captives nor cripples.

No subspecies recognized.

Aythya collaris (Donovan). Ring-necked Duck. Fairly common transient throughout state, rare winter resident.

No subspecies recognized.

Aythya valisineria (Wilson). Canvas-back. Fairly common transient and occasional winter resident throughout state.

No subspecies recognized.

Aythya marila. Greater Scaup Duck. Rare transient, status poorly known. Several sight records, one in winter. Floyd T. Amsden, a competent sportsman and amateur ornithologist of Wichita, identified 3 male specimens killed 3 miles north and 1 mile east of Sharon, Barber County, on October 27 (2) and November 3 (1), 1951. Frank Robl has seen specimens killed in Cheyenne Bottoms, Barton County. Every effort should be made to preserve specimens from Kansas.

Subspecies in Kansas: *A. m. nearctica* Stejneger, on geographical grounds.

Aythya affinis (Eyton). Lesser Scaup Duck. Common transient throughout state. A few records of wintering and summering (non-*breeding) individuals.

No subspecies recognized.

Bucephala clangula. Golden-eye. Uncommon transient and winter resident. Specimens from Kansas alleged to be the Barrow Golden-eye (*Bucephala islandica*) all are of the present species.

Subspecies in Kansas: *B. c. americana* (Bonaparte).

Bucephala albeola (Linnaeus). Buffle-head. Fairly common transient and occasional winter resident throughout state.

No subspecies recognized.

Clangula hyemalis (Linnaeus). Old-squaw. Rare transient and winter visitant. At least five specimens taken (but only two or three preserved) and numerous sight records, from widely separated parts of state.

No subspecies recognized.

Somateria mollissima. Eider. Accidental. One record: immature male (KU 3620), Kansas River near Lecompton, Douglas County, November 3, 1891, A. L. Wiedman.

Subspecies in Kansas: *S. m. v. nigra* Bonaparte (identification checked by A. Wetmore).

Somateria spectabilis (Linnaeus). King Eider. Accidental. One record: immature male (KU 27487), Kansas River 1 mile east of Lawrence, Douglas County, November 27, 1947, R. L. Montell.

No subspecies recognized.

Melanitta deglandi. White-winged Scoter. Rare transient. Nine specimens from Douglas and Leavenworth counties, taken from 1927 to 1938; several sight records from eastern Kansas.

Subspecies in Kansas: *M. d. deglandi* (Bonaparte).

Melanitta perspicillata (Linnaeus). Surf Scoter. Rare transient. Eight known specimens (three of which are now in University of Kansas collection), all taken in autumn, seven in Douglas County, one in Sedgwick County; several sight records from eastern Kansas.

No subspecies recognized.

Oidemia nigra. Common Scoter. Accidental. The two preserved specimens from Kansas supposedly of this species are actually Surf Scoters. L. B. Carson, however, identified an adult male Common Scoter killed by a hunter at Horton Lake, Brown County, in the early 1930's. Others have been seen by reliable field observers. Every effort should be made to secure specimens from Kansas.

Subspecies in Kansas: *O. n. americana* Swainson, on geographical grounds.

* *Oxyura jamaicensis.* Ruddy Duck. Common transient throughout state, rare winter resident. One breeding record: Frank Robl saw an adult female with one small young at Cheyenne Bottoms, Barton County, in approximately 1929.

Subspecies in Kansas: *O. j. rubida* (Wilson).

Lophodytes cucullatus (Linnaeus). Hooded Merganser. Uncommon transient and winter resident throughout state. Probably nests occasionally (two specimens at KU taken in east in June), but no proof of this available.

No subspecies recognized.

Mergus merganser. American Merganser. Common transient and winter resident throughout state.

Subspecies in Kansas: *M. m. americanus* Cassin.

Mergus serrator. Red-breasted Merganser. Uncommon transient throughout state; probably also rare winter resident but records lacking. This species is more common than Hooded Merganser in west, less common than Hooded in east.

Subspecies in Kansas: *M. s. serrator* Linnaeus.

* *Cathartes aura*. Turkey Vulture. Common transient throughout state; common summer resident west at least to Clark County. Breeding distribution in west poorly known.

Subspecies in Kansas: *C. a. teter* Friedmann.

Coragyps atratus (Meyer). Black Vulture. Once occurred in southeast, but no record since 1885. Goss quotes Dr. George Lisle ("a close observer") as finding this species common and breeding at Chetopa, Labette County, on the Oklahoma line, prior to 1883. Lisle found a nest with two eggs in 1858. Goss also reports one killed by Watson at Ellis, Ellis County, on March 27, 1885, but the location of the specimen is unknown. The species may still occur in southeastern Kansas.

No subspecies recognized.

* *Elanoïdes forficatus*. Swallow-tailed Kite. Formerly summer resident in at least eastern half of state. Last specimen from Kansas taken by Dr. G. C. Rinker at Hamilton, Greenwood County, May 17, 1914.

Subspecies in Kansas: *E. f. forficatus* (Linnaeus).

* *Ictinia misisippiensis* (Wilson). Mississippi Kite. Common summer resident in south-central Kansas, east to Harvey, north to Barton, and west to Kearny counties. Occasional records from Douglas (nested once), Johnson, Greenwood, and Hamilton counties.

No subspecies recognized.

Accipiter gentilis. Goshawk. Rare and irregular winter visitor in east. Status in west unknown.

Subspecies in Kansas: *A. g. atricapillus* (Wilson).

* *Accipiter striatus*. Sharp-shinned Hawk. Transient and winter resident throughout state; less common in east. Status in summer poorly known; one nest found in Cloud County, July 11, 1938, J. M. Porter.

Subspecies in Kansas: *A. s. velox* (Wilson).

* *Accipiter cooperii* (Bonaparte). Cooper Hawk. Resident throughout state but nesting records only from the eastern half, west to Cloud County.

No subspecies recognized.

* *Buteo jamaicensis*. Red-tailed Hawk. Abundant transient and winter resident in east; in High Plains of west, largely restricted to river bottoms in winter. Common summer resident in east; status in summer in west poorly known.

Subspecies in Kansas: *B. j. borealis* (Gmelin) is the breeding bird of eastern Kansas. *B. j. calurus* Cassin probably nests in west but no specimens available. *B.*

j. borealis, *B. j. calurus*, *B. j. kriderii* Hoopes, and *B. j. harlani* (Audubon), the latter considered here as conspecific with *jamaicensis*, all occur as transients and winter residents. More specimens needed to establish details of distribution of various subspecies.

* *Buteo lineatus*. Red-shouldered Hawk. Uncommon transient and summer resident and irregular winter resident in eastern Kansas. Breeding records from Leavenworth and Woodson counties; doubtless breeds in other eastern counties but definite evidence lacking.

Subspecies in Kansas: *B. l. lineatus* (Gmelin).

* *Buteo platypterus*. Broad-winged Hawk. Fairly common transient and local summer resident in eastern Kansas. Breeding records only from Douglas, Leavenworth, and Johnson counties, where species nests regularly.

Subspecies in Kansas: *B. p. platypterus* (Vieillot).

* *Buteo swainsoni* Bonaparte. Swainson Hawk. Abundant transient in west, fairly common in east. Nests commonly throughout western two-thirds of state and at least occasionally in eastern portion. Supposed winter records should be substantiated by specimens.

No subspecies recognized.

Buteo lagopus. Rough-legged Hawk. Winter resident, fairly common in east to common in west.

Subspecies in Kansas: *B. l. s. johannis* (Gmelin).

* *Buteo regalis* (Gray). Ferruginous Rough-leg. Common transient and winter resident in west, rare in east. Rare summer resident in west. Two nesting records: nest with four young, south fork of Smoky Hill River, near Wallace, May 27, 1883, Goss; nest with three young, west of Russell Springs, Logan County, May 29, 1954, Marvin D. Schwilling.

No subspecies recognized.

Parabuteo unicinctus. Harris Hawk. Accidental. Two records: male, Wichita, Sedgwick County, December 14, 1918, LeRoy Snyder; female (KU 10752), 7½ miles southwest of Lawrence, Douglas County, December 25, 1918, Fred Hastie.

Subspecies in Kansas: *P. u. harrisi* (Audubon).

* *Aquila chrysaëtos*. Golden Eagle. Formerly common resident throughout state. Now common in winter in west to rare in east. One positive nesting record: a pair nested for several years (prior to 1891) in southeastern Comanche County on a high gypsum ledge, Goss.

Subspecies in Kansas: *A. c. canadensis* (Linnaeus).

Haliaeetus leucocephalus. Bald Eagle. Rare transient and winter resident in east; fairly common winter resident in west, where large numbers may gather to roost.

Subspecies in Kansas: *H. l. alascanus* Townsend. Previous students refer all Bald Eagles from the state to *H. l. leucocephalus* (Linnaeus) but specimens in the K.

U. collection, all taken in winter, are large (three females, wing, 645, 655, 680 mm.) and are clearly of the northern subspecies.

Circus cyaneus. Marsh Hawk. Resident, common in winter, less common and local in summer.

Subspecies in Kansas: *C. c. hudsonius* (Linnaeus).

Pandion haliaetus. Osprey. Occurs irregularly throughout state but less frequently in west. Most records in spring and autumn but a few at other seasons. No definite nesting record.

Subspecies in Kansas: *P. h. carolinensis* (Gmelin).

Falco rusticolus. Gyrfalcon. Accidental. One specimen: Manhattan, Riley County, December 1, 1880, A. L. Runyan (specimen at Kansas State College).

Subspecies in Kansas: *F. r. obsoletus* Gmelin.

Falco mexicanus Schlegel. Prairie Falcon. Rare summer and fairly common winter resident in west; occasional transient and winter resident in east. No satisfactory breeding records.

No subspecies recognized.

* *Falco peregrinus.* Duck Hawk. Rare transient and winter resident, probably more common in west. Formerly nested but no nesting record since before 1900.

Subspecies in Kansas: *F. p. anatum* Bonaparte.

Falco columbarius. Pigeon Hawk. Uncommon transient and rare winter resident in east; more common in migration in west but status there in winter not known.

Subspecies in Kansas: *F. c. columbarius* Linnaeus is most frequent in eastern part, west to Reno County; *F. c. richardsonii* Ridgway is the common subspecies in west, occasional in east; *F. c. bendirei* Swann is known in Kansas from one specimen (KU 4425) from Ellis County, October, 1875, taken by Dr. L. Watson (identified by James L. Peters).

* *Falco sparverius.* Sparrow Hawk. Common resident and transient throughout state (but status in winter in northwest not known).

Subspecies in Kansas: *F. s. sparverius* Linnaeus.

Bonasa umbellus. Ruffed Grouse. Formerly common resident in eastern part; now probably extirpated in state but observers in extreme east should watch for it. One authentic specimen (KU 31944), southeastern Kansas, between 1885 and 1910, Alexander J. C. Roese. No definite nesting record.

Subspecies in Kansas: *B. u. umbellus* (Linnaeus).

* *Tympanuchus cupido.* Greater Prairie Chicken. Resident, but highly local; absent in southwestern quarter of state.

Subspecies in Kansas: *T. c. pinnatus* (Brewster).

* *Tympanuchus pallidicinctus* (Ridgway). Lesser Prairie Chicken. Resident, but local, in southwestern quarter of state, north to Hamilton and Finney counties

and east to Pawnee and Barber counties. A few old records east to Anderson and Neosho counties in winter.

No subspecies recognized.

Pedioecetes phasianellus. Sharp-tailed Grouse. Formerly resident in western part of state; scattered old records from eastern localities. Now extirpated, or nearly so, in Kansas; observers in northwestern counties should watch for it. No definite nesting record.

Subspecies in Kansas: *P. p. jamesi* Lincoln.

* *Colinus virginianus.* Bob-white. Resident, common in east, less common and local in west.

Subspecies in Kansas: *C. v. virginianus* (Linnaeus) in east, intergrading through central part with *C. v. taylori* Lincoln in west.

* *Callipepla squamata.* Scaled Quail. Locally common resident in southwest, formerly north to Wallace County but now primarily south of Arkansas River, eastern limit not known. Breeding records from Hamilton, Kearny, Finney, Stanton, Morton, Stevens, and Clark counties, Marvin D. Schwilling.

Subspecies in Kansas: *C. s. pallida* Brewster.

* *Phasianus colchicus* Linnaeus. Ring-necked Pheasant. Introduced. Common in western two-thirds, gradually invading east where a few are now found in most counties.

Origin of North American stock obscure; no subspecies now recognized here.

Meleagris gallopavo. Turkey. Formerly common resident, west along streams at least to Riley County; now extirpated in Kansas. No known specimen from Kansas with authentic data. No definite nesting record.

Subspecies in Kansas: *M. g. silvestris* Vieillot.

Grus americana (Linnaeus). Whooping Crane. Regular transient, now rare. Probably most individuals go through east-central part of state. Several early specimens from state and several recent sight records and one specimen: adult female (KU 31198), found crippled 8½ miles south of Sharon, Barber County, October 31, 1952, Thane S. Robinson.

No subspecies recognized.

Grus canadensis. Sandhill Crane. Transient, rare in east, common to abundant in west.

Subspecies in Kansas: *G. c. canadensis* (Linnaeus) and *G. c. tabida* (Peters); comparative status of the two subspecies not known.

* *Rallus elegans.* King Rail. Transient and summer resident, locally common.

Subspecies in Kansas: *R. e. elegans* Audubon.

Rallus limicola. Virginia Rail. Transient and summer resident, but breeding status poorly known. One breeding record: adult with six small, downy young, 8 miles south of Richfield, Morton County, May 24, 1950, Richard and Jean Graber.

Subspecies in Kansas: *R. l. limicola* Vieillot.

* *Porzana carolina* (Linnaeus). Sora. Common transient throughout state; status in summer poorly known. Two breeding records: Osawatomie, Miami County, prior to 1914 (no other details), record by Colvin, a careful observer; two nests, at least one with eggs, Finney County State Lake, August 21, 1951, Marvin D. Schwilling. Additional nesting records should be sought.

No subspecies recognized.

Coturnicops noveboracensis. Yellow Rail. Rare or generally overlooked transient. Records only from eastern part of state (west to Sedgwick County).

Subspecies in Kansas: *C. m. noveboracensis* (Gmelin).

* *Laterallus jamaicensis.* Black Rail. Rare or generally overlooked summer resident. At least ten records, including at least seven specimens from widely scattered localities. Two breeding records: nest with eight eggs, Manhattan, Riley County, June, 1880, C. P. Blachly; nest with nine eggs, near Garden City, Finney County, June 6, 1889, H. W. Menke.

Subspecies in Kansas: *L. j. jamaicensis* (Gmelin).

Porphyrula martinica (Linnaeus). Purple Gallinule. Rare and irregular summer visitant. Five specimens taken in April and June in Douglas, Sedgwick, and Riley counties. Several sight records from eastern Kansas.

No subspecies recognized.

* *Gallinula chloropus.* Florida Gallinule. Rare summer resident; status poorly known. Two breeding records: nest found "on a board," Coffey County, June (year not given), P. B. Peabody; nest (female, KU 27509, and two eggs taken), 3 miles northeast of Lawrence, Douglas County, May 22, 1945 (previously published as 1946), R. L. Montell.

Subspecies in Kansas: *G. c. cachinnans* Bangs.

* *Fulica americana.* American Coot. Uncommon summer resident, abundant transient, and local winter resident in east and central parts; status in west poorly known. Breeding record: 3 newly hatched young (KU 16694-6), Little Salt Marsh, Stafford County, June 13, 1927, H. C. Parker and W. H. Burt. The few other nesting localities include one in Finney County.

Subspecies in Kansas: *F. a. americana* Gmelin.

Charadrius hiaticula. Semipalmated Plover. Regular transient throughout state, often fairly common.

Subspecies in Kansas: *C. h. semipalmatus* Bonaparte.

Charadrius melodus. Piping Plover. Rare transient. Three specimens from Douglas County, March and April, and a female (KU 15492) from Little Salt Marsh, Stafford County, July 16, 1925, T. E. White. Nests in Nebraska, south at least to Lincoln; observers in north-central Kansas should watch for possible breeding birds.

Subspecies in Kansas: *C. m. circumcinctus* (Ridgway).

* *Charadrius alexandrinus.* Snowy Plover. Summer resident on salt plains of Clark, Comanche, Stafford, Barton, and probably other counties. Breeding range in Kansas poorly known. One definite nesting record: adults with young, and one nest with 3 eggs, Comanche County, June 18, 1886, Goss. One female (KU 7787), from Lawrence, Douglas County, April 22, 1909, L. L. Dyche.

Subspecies in Kansas: *C. a. tenuirostris* (Lawrence).

* *Charadrius vociferus.* Killdeer. Common transient and summer resident throughout state. Occasional winter resident.

Subspecies in Kansas: *C. v. vociferus* Linnaeus.

* *Eupoda montana* (Townsend). Mountain Plover. Summer resident in High Plains of western Kansas, but current status poorly known. Many specimens from west and one positive breeding record: two half-grown, partly downy males (KU 5512, 5513), 5 miles south of Tribune, Greeley County, June 21, 1911, Bunker and Rocklund.

No subspecies recognized.

Pluvialis dominica. Golden Plover. Regular transient in east, sometimes common; more common in spring than in autumn. Formerly abundant; status in west not known.

Subspecies in Kansas: *P. d. dominica* (Müller).

Squatarola squatarola (Linnaeus). Black-bellied Plover. Regular transient throughout state.

No subspecies recognized.

Arenaria interpres. Ruddy Turnstone. Rare transient. Several sight records from eastern part of state and two specimens: one killed at Topeka, Shawnee County, August 16, 1898, F. W. Forbes (location of specimen unknown); male, Hamilton, Greenwood County, October 1, 1911, G. C. Rinker.

Subspecies in Kansas: *A. i. morinella* (Linnaeus).

* *Philohela minor* (Gmelin). American Woodcock. Uncommon transient west to Scott and Kearny counties. Probably does not occur farther west. One early nesting record: adult with several "at least one-fourth grown" young, near Neosho Falls, Woodson County, May 25, 1874, Goss.

No subspecies recognized.

Capella gallinago. Wilson Snipe. Common transient and occasional winter resident throughout state.

Subspecies in Kansas: *C. g. delicata* (Ord).

* *Numenius americanus.* Long-billed Curlew. Transient and uncommon summer resident in west; occasional transient in east. Female and two downy young (KU 11607, 8, 9) taken 1 mile from Spring Creek, Morton County, June 27, 1927, W. H. Burt and L. V. Compton.

Subspecies in Kansas: *N. a. americanus* Bechstein is the breeding form; *N. a. par-*

vus Bishop occurs in migration (specimens from Riley, Lyon, and Douglas counties).

[*Numenius phaeopus*. Hudsonian Curlew. Reported by Goss, and one seen at Iatan Marsh, Atchison County, May 16, 1948, by Harold C. Hedges, but here placed in Hypothetical List until a specimen from Kansas is taken.]

Numenius borealis (Forster). Eskimo Curlew. Formerly abundant transient in eastern Kansas; now extinct, or nearly so. One unsexed bird (KU 6951) taken in Douglas County, May 6, 1873, by N. J. Stevens.

No subspecies recognized.

* *Bartramia longicauda* (Bechstein). Upland Plover. Abundant transient and locally common summer resident in suitable habitat; most numerous in west. Nesting records from Johnson, Wabaunsee, Chase, Finney, and Kearny counties.

No subspecies recognized.

* *Actitis macularia* (Linnaeus). Spotted Sandpiper. Common transient and summer resident throughout state. Breeding records from Leavenworth County and Kansas City region.

No subspecies recognized.

Tringa solitaria. Solitary Sandpiper. Common transient throughout state.

Subspecies in Kansas: *T. s. solitaria* Wilson is most common in eastern part and *T. s. cinnamomea* (Brewster) is most common in western part of Kansas, with much overlap of the two.

Catoptrophorus semipalmatus. Willet. Transient throughout state, usually uncommon, but sometimes locally common.

Subspecies in Kansas: *C. s. inornatus* (Brewster). *C. s. semipalmatus* (Gmelin) has been reported, probably erroneously; all specimens seen are of the western subspecies, *inornatus*.

Totanus melanoleucus (Gmelin). Greater Yellow-legs. Common transient throughout state.

No subspecies recognized.

Totanus flavipes (Gmelin). Lesser Yellow-legs. Common transient throughout state.

No subspecies recognized.

Calidris canutus. American Knot. Rare transient. Sight records from eastern and western Kansas; only one specimen preserved, Hamilton, Greenwood County, September 19, 1911, G. C. Rinker.

Subspecies in Kansas: *C. c. rufa* (Wilson).

Erolia melanotos (Vieillot). Pectoral Sandpiper. Common transient through state.

No subspecies recognized.

Erolia fuscicollis (Vieillot). White-rumped Sandpiper. Common transient throughout state.

No subspecies recognized.

Erolia bairdii (Coues). Baird Sandpiper. Common transient in east; abundant transient in west.

No subspecies recognized.

Erolia minutilla (Vieillot). Least Sandpiper. Common transient throughout state, but less numerous in west than in east.

No subspecies recognized.

Erolia alpina. Red-backed Sandpiper. Rare or uncommon transient; reported only from eastern half of state, west to Cloud County. Few specimens have been preserved.

Subspecies in Kansas: *E. a. pacifica* (Coues).

Limnodromus griseus. Short-billed Dowitcher. Rare or uncommon transient in east, status in west not known. One specimen: male (KU 29403), 3 miles east of Lawrence, Douglas County, May 14, 1946, R. L. Montell. Dowitchers having noticeably short bills should be collected when possible.

Subspecies in Kansas: *L. g. hendersoni* Rowan.

Limnodromus scolopaceus (Say). Long-billed Dowitcher. Common transient throughout state.

No subspecies recognized.

Micropalama himantopus (Bonaparte). Stilt Sandpiper. Common transient throughout state.

No subspecies recognized.

Ereunetes pusillus (Linnaeus). Semipalmated Sandpiper. Common transient throughout state.

No subspecies recognized.

Ereunetes mauri Cabanis. Western Sandpiper. Uncommon transient in east; probably common in west but status there unknown.

No subspecies recognized.

Tryngites subruficollis (Vieillot). Buff-breasted Sandpiper. Uncommon but regular transient in autumn in eastern Kansas, west to Republic County; few spring records.

No subspecies recognized.

Limosa fedoa (Linnaeus). Marbled Godwit. Rare or uncommon transient throughout state. Status somewhat uncertain because some observers confuse this species with female Hudsonian Godwits. The latter are larger and often much duller than male Hudsonian Godwits. Marbled Godwits, however, show no contrasting tail pattern in flight.

No subspecies recognized.

Limosa haemastica (Linnaeus). Hudsonian Godwit. Uncommon transient in eastern and central Kansas; status in west poorly known (reported from Ness and Kearny counties).

No subspecies recognized.

Crocethia alba (Pallas). Sanderling. Rare transient in eastern and central Kansas; status in west not known. Three specimens have been taken, two from Douglas County (October) and one from Stafford County (July).

No subspecies recognized.

* *Recurvirostra americana* Gmelin. Avocet. Uncommon transient in east; common transient and uncommon summer resident in west. Breeding records from Kearny, Finney, Haskell, Meade, and Barton counties.

No subspecies recognized.

Himantopus mexicanus (Müller). Black-necked Stilt. Rare transient. Records from Crawford, Sedgwick, Cloud, Stafford, Finney, and Kearny counties; few recent records. No satisfactory nesting record.

No subspecies recognized.

Phalaropus fulicarius (Linnaeus). Red Phalarope. Very rare transient. Two specimens: female (KU 3778), Lake View, Douglas County, November 5, 1905, E. E. Brown; male (Ottawa Univ. 96), near Ottawa, Franklin County, October 25, 1926, Wesley Clanton (identification checked by Tordoff).

No subspecies recognized.

* *Steganopus tricolor* Vieillot. Wilson Phalarope. Common transient throughout state. One definite nesting record: adult male with downy young, Cheyenne Bottoms, Barton County, June 26, 1954, Ted F. Andrews and Homer Stephens. Goss mentioned "breeding birds" in Meade County but the record is not convincing.

No subspecies recognized.

Lobipes lobatus (Linnaeus). Northern Phalarope. Rare transient. Goss shot five and preserved one (now in Goss collection) of 17 or 18 seen at Fort Wallace, Wallace County, May 25, 1883. Several sight records.

No subspecies recognized.

Stercorarius pomarinus (Temminck). Pomarine Jaeger. Accidental. One record: immature male (KU 6967), Kansas River near Lawrence, Douglas County, October 10, 1898, Gus Berger and Banks Brown. This specimen erroneously reported as a Parasitic Jaeger, *Stercorarius parasiticus* (Linnaeus), in previous lists of birds of Kansas.

No subspecies recognized.

Stercorarius longicaudus Vieillot. Long-tailed Jaeger. Accidental. One record: female (KU 32610), Cheyenne Bottoms, Barton County, June 23, 1955, William M. Lynn and Larry D. Mosby.

No subspecies recognized.

[*Larus hyperboreus*. Glaucous Gull. One bird with crippled leg seen at Lake Shawnee, Shawnee County, January 27, 1951, and several days thereafter, by many observers including the author. Placed on Hypothetical List until specimen is taken in Kansas.]

Larus argentatus. Herring Gull. Transient, regular along Missouri River, uncommon to rare elsewhere in state; probably rare winter resident.

Subspecies in Kansas: *L. a. smithsonianus* Coues.

Larus californicus Lawrence. California Gull. Accidental. One record: specimen (location unknown) taken by Goss, Arkansas River, Reno County, October 20, 1880.

No subspecies recognized.

Larus delawarensis Ord. Ring-billed Gull. Transient, locally common; rare winter resident.

No subspecies recognized.

Larus atricilla Linnaeus. Laughing Gull. Accidental. One specimen taken 3 miles east and 2½ miles south of Canton, in Marion County, May 15, 1933, Richard H. Schmidt (specimen in his collection); sight records from Barton and Shawnee counties.

No subspecies recognized.

Larus pipixcan Wagler. Franklin Gull. Transient, abundant in west, common in east.

No subspecies recognized.

Larus philadelphia (Ord). Bonaparte Gull. Rare transient. All specimens from eastern part, west to Cloud County; status in west not known.

No subspecies recognized.

[*Rissa tridactyla*. Kittiwake. Immature bird seen at Lake Shawnee, Shawnee County, October 20, 1951, by L. B. Carson and O. S. Pettingill, Jr. In the absence of a specimen, the species is placed on the Hypothical List.]

Xema sabini. Sabine Gull. Three records: immature male, taken at Humboldt, Allen County, September 19, 1876, Peter Long (now in Goss collection); immature male, taken at Hamilton, Greenwood County, October 3, 1909, G. C. Rinker; immature bird seen but not collected on October 18, 28, and 29, 1952, at Lake Shawnee, Shawnee County, by several observers (Orville O. Rice secured good photographs of this bird).

Subspecies in Kansas: *X. s. sabini* (Sabine).

Sterna forsteri Nuttall. Forster Tern. Transient, locally common in eastern half of state; status in west unknown.

No subspecies recognized.

Sterna hirundo. Common Tern. Rare transient. Two specimens: female, Anderson County, May 11, 1878 (in Goss collection); male, Munger's Lake, near Hamilton, Greenwood County, September 2, 1912, G. C. Rinker.

Subspecies in Kansas: *S. h. hirundo* Linnaeus.

* *Sterna albifrons.* Least Tern. Uncommon transient and local summer resident throughout state. One definite nesting record: five nests, each with two eggs, Arkansas River at Coolidge, Hamilton County, July 1, 1936, Otto Tiemeier.

Subspecies in Kansas: *S. a. athalassos* Burleigh and Lowery.

Hydroprogne caspia (Pallas). Caspian Tern. Uncommon transient throughout state. Many sight records but only one specimen: female (KU 17147), Douglas County, September 27, 1928, Harold Standing (skin and body skeleton of this tern saved; erroneously reported previously as two specimens).

No subspecies recognized.

Chlidonias niger. Black Tern. Common transient and, in north-central part, regular summer resident but no positive breeding record.

Subspecies in Kansas: *C. n. surinamensis* (Gmelin).

* *Columba livia* Gmelin. Rock Dove. Introduced. Common around habitations; nesting locally in feral state on cliffs in western Kansas.

No subspecies recognized because of mixed ancestry of birds introduced into New World.

* *Zenaidura macroura.* Mourning Dove. Common transient and summer resident, uncommon winter resident.

Subspecies in Kansas: *Z. m. carolinensis* (Linnaeus) in east, *Z. m. marginella* (Woodhouse) in west, intergrading in central part.

* *Ectopistes migratorius* (Linnaeus). Passenger Pigeon. Extinct. Formerly irregular transient and summer resident. Two specimens, both males, taken at Neosho Falls, Woodson County, April 14, 1876, by Goss, who also reported this species to nest there occasionally.

No subspecies recognized.

[*Columbigallina passerina.* Ground Dove. One seen on Kansas River, 3 miles west of St. Marys, Pottawatomie County, November 11, 1954, by Thomas A. Hoffman and James Mulligan. Placed in Hypothetical List in absence of a specimen from Kansas.]

[*Scardafella inca* (Lesson). Inca Dove. One seen daily at Halstead, Harvey County, November 10, 1951, to January 21, 1952, by Edna L. Ruth and others. One seen in Topeka, Shawnee County, last week of June, 1952, E. J. Rice. Placed in Hypothetical List in absence of a specimen from Kansas.]

* *Conuropsis carolinensis.* Carolina Paroquet. Extinct. Formerly common resident in wooded areas of east; west along stream bottoms. Goss reported nesting of small flock near Neosho Falls, Woodson County, in spring, 1858. No specimen

from Kansas preserved.

Subspecies in Kansas: *C. c. ludovicianus* (Gmelin), on geographical grounds.

* *Coccyzus americanus.* Yellow-billed Cuckoo. Common transient and summer resident throughout state.

Subspecies in Kansas: *C. a. americanus* (Linnaeus).

* *Coccyzus erythropthalmus* (Wilson). Black-billed Cuckoo. Uncommon transient and summer resident. Nesting records: female (KU 15480) and nest containing two Black-billed Cuckoo eggs and one Yellow-billed Cuckoo egg, 7½ miles southwest of Lawrence, Douglas County, June 5, 1926, Charles D. Bunker; nests found in Cloud County in June, 1932 (1), 1933 (1), 1934 (1), 1935 (1), 1938 (2), J. M. Porter.

No subspecies recognized.

* *Geococcyx californianus* (Lesson). Road-runner. Resident in south-central and southwestern Kansas; abundance and distribution subject to wide fluctuation, current status unknown. Four nests found, April to July, 1934, 4½ miles east of Arkansas City, Cowley County, Walter Colvin.

No subspecies recognized.

Crotophaga sulcirostris. Groove-billed Ani. Accidental. Three records: specimen (KU 31948), McCune, Crawford County, between 1885 and 1910, Alexander J. C. Roese; specimen, Lyon County, November 1, 1904; male (KU 31951), 6¾ miles northeast of Blue Rapids, Marshall County, October 28, 1952, Elizabeth G. McCleod.

Subspecies in Kansas: *C. s. sulcirostris* Swainson.

* *Tyto alba.* Barn owl. Uncommon resident throughout state.

Subspecies in Kansas: *T. a. pratincola* (Bonaparte).

* *Otus asio.* Screech Owl. Common resident throughout state.

Subspecies in Kansas: Following reported: *O. a. naevius* (Gmelin) in northeast, *O. a. hasbroucki* Ridgway in south-central, *O. a. aikeni* (Brewster) and *O. a. swenki* Oberholser in west. The status of these subspecies is poorly known; additional breeding specimens and revisionary study are needed.

* *Bubo virginianus.* Horned Owl. Common resident throughout state.

Subspecies in Kansas: *B. v. virginianus* (Gmelin) in east, *B. v. occidentalis* Stone in west.

Nyctea scandiaca (Linnaeus). Snowy Owl. Rare and irregular winter visitant throughout state.

No subspecies recognized.

[*Surnia ulula.* Hawk Owl. None of the several sight records from Kansas is convincing to me. Reports from eastern Kansas indicating regular occurrence there of this far-northern species are surely erroneous and probably pertain to Short-eared Owls.]

* *Speotyto cunicularia.* Burrowing Owl. Common summer resident in west; irregular transient in east. Numbers seem to be decreasing.

Subspecies in Kansas: *S. c. hypugea* (Bonaparte).

* *Strix varia.* Barred Owl. Resident in east, locally fairly common. Status in west not known.

Subspecies in Kansas: *S. v. georgica* Latham in southeast; *S. v. varia* Barton elsewhere in state.

* *Asio otus.* Long-eared Owl. Uncommon summer resident, locally common transient and winter resident throughout state. Nesting records from Ottawa, Douglas, Doniphan, and Meade counties. Status in summer poorly known.

Subspecies in Kansas: *A. o. wilsonianus* (Lesson).

* *Asio flammeus.* Short-eared Owl. Resident, probably throughout state, in suitable habitat. More common in winter. Nesting records from Woodson, Republic, and Marshall counties.

Subspecies in Kansas: *A. f. flammeus* (Pontoppidan).

* *Aegolius acadicus.* Saw-whet Owl. Rare winter resident throughout state. One nesting record: a pair found in Kansas City, Wyandotte County, in winter, 1950, remained at least to September, 1951, and were seen with young birds in summer, 1951, John Bishop.

Subspecies in Kansas: *A. a. acadicus* (Gmelin).

* *Caprimulgus carolinensis* Gmelin. Chuck-will's-widow. Locally common summer resident in eastern Kansas, western limit of distribution poorly known.

No subspecies recognized.

* *Caprimulgus vociferus.* Whip-poor-will. Locally common summer resident in eastern Kansas; two specimens reported from Finney County, but status in west poorly known. Two nests reported, at Geary, Doniphan County, June 16 and June 14 to July 3, 1923, by Linsdale. In recent years, Chuck-will's-widows seem to have increased at the expense of Whip-poor-wills in Kansas.

Subspecies in Kansas: *C. v. vociferus* Wilson.

* *Phalaenoptilus nuttallii.* Poor-will. Summer resident, common in west, rare and local in east.

Subspecies in Kansas: *P. n. nuttallii* (Audubon).

* *Chordeiles minor.* Nighthawk. Common transient and summer resident throughout state.

Subspecies in Kansas: Nesting; *C. m. minor* (Forster) in northeast, *C. m. chapmani* Coues in southeast, and *C. m. howelli* Oberholser in west, intergrading with one another through fairly broad zones. Migration; *C. m. sennetti* Coues throughout state.

* *Chaetura pelagica* (Linnaeus). Chimney Swift. Common transient and summer resident in east; status in west poorly known. Schwilling reports this species only

in migration in Finney and neighboring counties.

No subspecies recognized.

* *Archilochus colubris* (Linnaeus). Ruby-throated Hummingbird. Common transient and summer resident in east; much less common in west, status there poorly known.

No subspecies recognized.

Stellula calliope (Gould). Calliope Hummingbird. One record: immature female, 8 miles south of Richfield and 6 miles east of Kansas Highway 27, Morton County, September 3, 1952, Jean W. Graber.

No subspecies recognized.

* *Megaceryle alcyon.* Belted Kingfisher. Common summer resident and uncommon winter resident throughout state.

Subspecies in Kansas: *M. a. alcyon* (Linnaeus).

* *Colaptes auratus.* Yellow-shafted Flicker. Common resident throughout state, but partly replaced in west by Red-shafted Flicker and hybrids between the two species.

Subspecies in Kansas: *C. a. auratus* (Linnaeus) in southeast, *C. a. luteus* Bangs in remainder of state. *C. a. borealis* Ridgway has been reported in winter in east.

* *Colaptes cafer.* Red-shafted Flicker. Common resident in west, hybridizing with, and replaced by, Yellow-shafted Flicker eastward. Uncommon winter resident in east.

Subspecies in Kansas: *C. c. collaris* Vigors.

* *Dryocopus pileatus.* Pileated Woodpecker. Formerly common resident in eastern Kansas, now much reduced in numbers and distribution. Recent sight records from Leavenworth, Wyandotte, Douglas, Miami, Linn, and Neosho counties may indicate that this species is increasing in its former range. Definite nesting records only from Linn County where Frank Wood and Ivan Sutton found a nest with 4 eggs and a nest with two young and one egg, along Marais des Cygnes River, near Pleasanton, some years ago. Eunice and Wilson Dingus have noted this species at Mound City, Linn County, regularly for several years.

Subspecies in Kansas: *D. p. abieticola* (Bangs) in northeast, *D. p. pileatus* (Linnaeus) in southeast.

* *Centurus carolinus.* Red-bellied Woodpecker. Common resident in eastern part, breeding west at least to Comanche County; additional records in west from Morton, Finney, and Kearny counties.

Subspecies in Kansas: *C. c. zebra* (Boddaert).

* *Melanerpes erythrocephalus.* Red-headed Woodpecker. Common transient and summer resident throughout state. Occasional winter resident west to Cloud County; not found in winter in southwest by Schwilling.

Subspecies in Kansas: *M. e. erythrocephalus* (Linnaeus), intergrading in west with *M. e. caurinus* Brodkorb.

Asyndesmus lewis (Gray). Lewis Woodpecker. Possibly rare resident in southwest but status uncertain. Several specimens and sight records from western third of state; one specimen, female (KU 7890), from Lawrence, Douglas County, November 7, 1908, Bunker and Wetmore.

No subspecies recognized.

Sphyrapicus varius. Yellow-bellied Sapsucker. Uncommon transient and winter resident throughout state.

Subspecies in Kansas: *S. v. varius* (Linnaeus) in eastern Kansas, *S. v. nuchalis* Baird in western part (three specimens, Wallace and Morton counties).

[*Sphyrapicus thyroideus.* Williamson Sapsucker. An adult male seen at Concordia, Cloud County, April 4, 1935, by Dr. J. M. Porter. Placed in Hypothetical List in absence of a specimen.]

* *Dendrocopos villosus.* Hairy Woodpecker. Common resident throughout state.

Subspecies in Kansas: *D. v. villosus* (Linnaeus).

* *Dendrocopos pubescens.* Downy Woodpecker. Common resident throughout state.

Subspecies in Kansas: *D. p. pubescens* (Linnaeus) in southeast (Labette and Montgomery counties), *D. p. medianus* (Swainson) in rest of state, with fairly broad zone of intergradation between the two subspecies.

Dendrocopos scalaris. Ladder-backed Woodpecker. Common resident in extreme southwestern Kansas (Morton County). Six specimens. No nest found yet in Kansas.

Subspecies in Kansas: *D. s. symplectus* (Oberholser).

* *Tyrannus tyrannus* (Linnaeus). Eastern Kingbird. Common transient and summer resident throughout state; most numerous in east.

No subspecies recognized.

* *Tyrannus verticalis* Say. Western Kingbird. Common transient and summer resident east to Flint Hills; uncommon transient and summer resident in east (occurs regularly at Lawrence but rarely at Kansas City).

No subspecies recognized.

Tyrannus vociferans. Cassin Kingbird. Transient and summer resident in extreme western part, east to Finney County. One specimen: male, Kansas Highway 27 at Cimarron River [7½ miles north of Elkhart], Morton County, May 26, 1950, Richard and Jean Graber. No nesting record. Status poorly known.

Subspecies in Kansas: *T. v. vociferans* Swainson.

* *Muscivora forficata* (Gmelin). Scissor-tailed Flycatcher. Common summer resident in southern and central Kansas; nesting west to Morton County, north to Cloud County, east to Neosho County. Sporadic records elsewhere in state.

No subspecies recognized.

* *Myiarchus crinitus*. Crested Flycatcher. Common transient and summer resident throughout state, but perhaps less numerous in west.

Subspecies in Kansas: *M. c. boreus* Bangs.

Myiarchus cinerascens. Ash-throated Flycatcher. Known only from Morton County; several seen in May, 1950, and a female with somewhat enlarged ovary taken, 8 miles south of Richfield, May 7, 1950, Richard and Jean Graber. No nesting record.

Subspecies in Kansas: *M. c. cinerascens* (Lawrence).

* *Sayornis phoebe* (Latham). Eastern Phoebe. Common transient and summer resident in east; occurs, but must less common, in west.

No subspecies recognized.

* *Sayornis saya*. Say Phoebe. Common transient and summer resident in west. Nesting records from Rawlins, Jewell, Logan, and Ness counties. In migration, reported east to Republic and Lyon counties.

Subspecies in Kansas: *S. s. saya* (Bonaparte) is the breeding bird; *S. s. yukonensis* Bishop probably occurs in migration.

Empidonax flaviventris (Baird and Baird). Yellow-bellied Flycatcher. Uncommon transient in east. Specimens from Johnson, Douglas, and Shawnee counties.

No subspecies recognized.

* *Empidonax virescens* (Vieillot). Acadian Flycatcher. Summer resident in eastern Kansas. Specimens from Doniphan, Leavenworth, Douglas, Woodson, Montgomery, and Labette counties. Nesting records from Doniphan County (Jean M. Linsdale), Linn County (Wilson J. and Eunice Dingus), and Douglas County (R. F. Miller).

No subspecies recognized.

Empidonax traillii. Alder Flycatcher. Transient throughout state; no satisfactory nesting records or specimens taken in breeding season.

Subspecies in Kansas: *E. t. brewsteri* Oberholser transient, probably more common in west, and *E. t. traillii* (Audubon) transient and perhaps breeding in east.

Empidonax minimus (Baird and Baird). Least Flycatcher. Common transient throughout state; no satisfactory evidence of nesting.

No subspecies recognized.

Empidonax oberholseri Phillips. Wright Flycatcher. Known only from three specimens, May 8 (male and female) and May 12 (male), 1950, eight miles south of Richfield, Morton County, Richard and Jean Graber.

No subspecies recognized.

Empidonax difficilis. Western Flycatcher. Known only from two specimens taken eight miles south of Richfield, Morton County; September 3, 1952, immature female, Jean Graber; September 5, 1952, immature male (KU 31203), Richard Graber.

Subspecies in Kansas: *E. d. hellmayri* Brodkorb (female specimen); intermediate between *E. d. hellmayri* and *E. d. difficilis* Baird (male specimen).

* *Contopus virens* (Linnaeus). Eastern Wood Pewee. Common transient and summer resident in east, rare transient in west. Breeding distribution in state poorly known.

No subspecies recognized.

Contopus richardsonii. Western Wood Pewee. Common transient and probably summer resident in west; rare transient in east (specimen from Greenwood County and one seen in Cloud County). No nesting record.

Subspecies in Kansas: *C. r. richardsonii* (Swainson).

Nuttallornis borealis (Swainson). Olive-sided Flycatcher. Uncommon transient throughout state.

No subspecies recognized.

* *Eremophila alpestris.* Horned Lark. Common transient and resident throughout state. Numbers augmented by northern birds in winter.

Subspecies in Kansas: *E. a. praticola* (Henshaw) resident in east; *E. a. enthymia* (Oberholser) resident west of Flint Hills; *E. a. hoyti* (Bishop), *E. a. alpestris* (Linnaeus), and *E. a. leucolaema* (Coues) in winter.

[*Tachycineta thalassina.* Violet-green Swallow. Five birds seen at Lake Shawnee, Shawnee County, April 14, 1947, by L. B. Carson. Placed in Hypothetical List in absence of a specimen.]

* *Iridoprocne bicolor* (Vieillot). Tree Swallow. Summer resident in extreme northeastern Kansas; common transient throughout eastern half of state, status in west not known. Nesting records only from Doniphan County, along Missouri River, four nests located by Linsdale, in 1922, 1923, and 1924, and Leavenworth County, nests found by Brumwell along Missouri River.

No subspecies recognized.

* *Riparia riparia.* Bank Swallow. Common transient and summer resident, probably throughout state but status in northwest not known.

Subspecies in Kansas: *R. r. riparia* (Linnaeus).

* *Stelgidopteryx ruficollis.* Rough-winged Swallow. Common transient and summer resident throughout state.

Subspecies in Kansas: *S. r. serripennis* (Audubon).

* *Hirundo rustica.* Barn Swallow. Common transient and summer resident throughout state.

Subspecies in Kansas: *H. r. erythrogaster* Boddaert.

* *Petrochelidon pyrrhonota.* Cliff Swallow. Common transient and locally common summer resident throughout state.

Subspecies in Kansas: *P. p. pyrrhonota* (Vieillot).

Progne subis. Purple Martin. Common transient and summer resident in east to uncommon or rare in west.

Subspecies in Kansas: *P. s. subis* (Linnaeus).

* *Cyanocitta cristata.* Blue Jay. Common transient and resident throughout state; less common in northern and western sections in winter.

Subspecies in Kansas: *C. c. bromia* Oberholser in east, *C. c. cyanotephra* Sutton in west, intergrading through central Kansas.

[*Cyanocitta stelleri.* Steller Jay. Several sight records from southwestern Kansas. Placed in Hypothetical List in absence of a specimen.]

Aphelocoma coerulescens. Scrub Jay. Irregular winter resident in southwestern Kansas. Five specimens (KU 20812-5, 21213), 12 miles northeast of Elkhart, Morton County, November 8, 10, 14, 1934, W. S. Long and Fred Hastie. Two seen in Finney County, January 15, 1955, by Marvin D. Schwilling.

Subspecies in Kansas: *A. c. woodhouseii* (Baird).

Aphelocoma ultramarina. Arizona Jay. Accidental. One specimen: "probably female," near Mt. Jesus, Clark County, March, 1906, B. Ashton Keith. Identification confirmed by L. L. Dyche; present location of specimen unknown.

Subspecies in Kansas: *A. u. arizonae* (Ridgway).

* *Pica pica.* American Magpie. Common resident in west; occasional in east in winter. Eastward extent of breeding range poorly known; nests from Ottawa (1951), Republic (1951 and 1953), and Cloud (1954) counties. Extending breeding range eastward (J. M. Porter).

Subspecies in Kansas: *P. p. hudsonia* (Sabine).

Corvus corax. American Raven. Formerly occurred on High Plains, precise status not known. No records since disappearance of bison herds. One specimen: Jewell County, date unknown, Edward Kern (specimen now at Kansas State College, Manhattan).

Subspecies in Kansas: *C. c. sinuatus* Wagler.

* *Corvus cryptoleucus* Couch. White-necked Raven. Common summer resident in western two tiers of counties; occasional resident east to Ford County. Locally common winter resident (Finney, Scott, and Sherman counties). One shot at Larned, Pawnee County, about October 25, 1937, by Frank Robl.

No subspecies recognized.

* *Corvus brachyrhynchos.* Crow. Common resident in east, less common in west. Abundant transient and winter resident in central Kansas.

Subspecies in Kansas: *C. b. brachyrhynchos* Brehm.

Gymnorhinus cyanocephalus Wied. Piñon Jay. Irregular winter visitant, more frequent in west than in east. Reported from Douglas (twice), Sedgwick, Mitchell, Clark, Finney, and Kearny counties.

No subspecies recognized.

Nucifraga columbiana (Wilson). Clark Nutcracker. Irregular winter visitant, more frequent in west than in east. Reported from Marshall (twice), Ellis, Lyon, Finney, and Seward counties.

No subspecies recognized.

* *Parus atricapillus*. Black-capped Chickadee. Common resident in entire state except for southern tier of counties, where either rare or absent in summer and locally common in winter.

Subspecies in Kansas: *P. a. atricapillus* Linnaeus in east, where most specimens are more or less intermediate toward *P. a. septentrionalis* Harris, the resident subspecies in the west.

* *Parus carolinensis*. Carolina Chickadee. Common resident in southern tier of counties; taken also in Greenwood County. Reported occurrence in Douglas County is erroneous. Proof of breeding rests on partly grown juveniles taken in Barber County, and on two nests found in Montgomery County by L. B. Carson.

Subspecies in Kansas: *P. c. atricapilloides* Lunk.

* *Parus bicolor* Linnaeus. Tufted Titmouse. Common resident in eastern Kansas, west at least to Barber, Harvey, and Cloud counties. Western limit of breeding range poorly known.

No subspecies recognized.

* *Sitta carolinensis*. White-breasted Nuthatch. Uncommon and local resident and winter visitant throughout state. Three positive nesting records, all from Douglas County, by C. D. Bunker, R. F. Miller, and Katherine Kelley.

Subspecies in Kansas: *S. c. carolinensis* Latham resident in Labette and Montgomery counties; *S. c. nelsoni* Mearns occurs in at least Morton County, status uncertain; *S. c. cookei* Oberholser resident and winter visitant in rest of state.

Sitta canadensis Linnaeus. Red-breasted Nuthatch. Uncommon transient and winter resident throughout state.

No subspecies recognized.

Certhia familiaris. Brown Creeper. Fairly common transient and winter resident throughout state.

Subspecies in Kansas: *C. f. americana* Bonaparte.

* *Troglodytes aëdon*. House Wren. Transient and summer resident, common in east to uncommon in west.

Subspecies in Kansas: *T. a. parkmanii* Audubon.

Troglodytes troglodytes. Winter Wren. Rare or uncommon transient and winter resident throughout state.

Subspecies in Kansas: *T. t. hiemalis* Vieillot.

Thryomanes bewickii. Bewick Wren. Resident, common in south, rare in north;

status poorly known. Nesting records from Shawnee, Johnson, and Montgomery counties.

Subspecies in Kansas: *T. b. bewickii* (Audubon) in northern and northeastern part, *T. b. cryptus* Oberholser in rest of state. (*T. b. niceae* Sutton, a questionably valid subspecies, has been reported from Meade and Morton counties.)

* *Thryothorus ludovicianus.* Carolina Wren. Resident, common in south, less common to north and west. One record from Hamilton County; status in northwest unknown.

Subspecies in Kansas: *T. l. ludovicianus* (Latham).

* *Telmatodytes palustris.* Long-billed Marsh Wren. Uncommon transient throughout state; known as a breeding bird only from Doniphan County, where Linsdale found several nests and collected a juvenile (KU 12869) with half-grown tail, August 31, 1922.

Subspecies in Kansas: *T. p. dissaëptus* (Bangs).

* *Cistothorus platensis.* Short-billed Marsh Wren. Uncommon transient and irregular summer resident in east, no records from west. One breeding record: male (KU 29665), female (KU 29666), and their nest with four eggs, eight miles west of Lawrence, Douglas County, August 30, 1950, H. B. Tordoff and G. P. Young.

Subspecies in Kansas: *C. p. stellaris* (Naumann).

* *Salpinctes obsoletus.* Rock Wren. Common transient and summer resident in west, rare transient in east; eastern limit of breeding range not known. Nests found in Hamilton, Scott, and Logan counties.

Subspecies in Kansas: *S. o. obsoletus* (Say).

* *Mimus polyglottos.* Mockingbird. Resident throughout state, less common in north, especially in winter.

Subspecies in Kansas: *M. p. polyglottos* (Linnaeus) in east, *M. p. leucopterus* (Vigors) in west (most specimens from Kansas are intermediate between the two subspecies).

* *Dumetella carolinensis* (Linnaeus). Catbird. Common transient and summer resident throughout state.

No subspecies recognized.

* *Toxostoma rufum.* Brown Thrasher. Common transient and summer resident throughout state; occasional winter resident at least in east.

Subspecies in Kansas: *T. r. rufum* (Linnaeus) in east, *T. r. longicauda* Baird in west.

Oreoscoptes montanus (Townsend). Sage Thrasher. Rare transient in west. Two unsexed specimens (KU 31941, 31942), 1 mile south of Holcomb, Finney County, September 20 and October 2, 1954, Marvin D. Schwilling. A third individual seen in Morton County, September 27, 1954, and a fourth in Kearny County, March 23, 1955, by Schwilling.

No subspecies recognized.

* *Turdus migratorius.* Robin. Common transient and summer resident; locally common winter resident.

Subspecies in Kansas: *T. m. migratorius* Linnaeus breeds in most of state but birds in southeast are intermediate toward *T. m. achrusterus* (Batchelder); *T. m. propinquus* Ridgway occurs in west, at least in migration, and irregularly in other parts of state in winter.

Ixoreus naevius. Varied Thrush. Accidental. One record: specimen (present location unknown) taken at Garden City, Finney County, October 17, 1891, H. W. Menke.

Subspecies in Kansas: Probably *I. n. meruloides* (Swainson), on geographical grounds.

* *Hylocichla mustelina* (Gmelin). Wood Thrush. Common transient and summer resident in east, absent in west, western limit of breeding in Kansas not known (nests, but uncommonly, in Cloud County).

No subspecies recognized.

Hylocichla guttata. Hermit Thrush. Transient throughout state, usually uncommon. Rare in winter in east.

Subspecies in Kansas: *H. g. faxoni* Bangs and Penard in east, *H. g. sequoiensis* (Belding) in west.

Hylocichla ustulata. Olive-backed Thrush. Common transient throughout state.

Subspecies in Kansas: *H. u. swainsoni* (Tschudi).

Hylocichla minima. Gray-cheeked Thrush. Fairly common transient in east; probably does not occur in west but western limit in migration in Kansas unknown (rare in Cloud County, three records by J. M. Porter).

Subspecies in Kansas: *H. m. minima* (Lafresnaye).

Hylocichla fuscescens. Veery. Transient, rare in east, fairly common in west.

Subspecies in Kansas: *H. f. salicicola* Ridgway.

* *Sialia sialis.* Eastern Bluebird. Common resident and transient throughout state.

Subspecies in Kansas: *S. s. sialis* (Linnaeus).

[*Sialia mexicana.* Chestnut-backed Bluebird. Said to be winter resident at Coolidge, Hamilton County, by Shanstrum. Reliably reported from southeastern Colorado. Placed in Hypothetical List in absence of a specimen from Kansas.]

Sialia currucoides (Bechstein). Mountain Bluebird. Common winter resident in west; occurs regularly east to Cloud and Barber counties and irregularly farther east (to Douglas and Anderson counties). Bunker and Rocklund took a full-grown juvenal female (KU 5900) on June 20, 1911, near the Colorado line northwest of Coolidge, Hamilton County.

No subspecies recognized.

Myadestes townsendi. Townsend Solitaire. Winter resident in small numbers in west; irregular in winter in east.

Subspecies in Kansas: *M. t. townsendi* (Audubon).

* *Polioptila caerulea.* Blue-gray Gnatcatcher. Common transient and summer resident in east, probably transient only in west but status there poorly known. Nesting records from Doniphan, Douglas, and Barber counties.

Subspecies in Kansas: *P. c. caerulea* (Linnaeus).

Regulus satrapa. Golden-crowned Kinglet. Common transient throughout state; uncommon winter resident.

Subspecies in Kansas: *R. s. satrapa* Lichtenstein.

Regulus calendula. Ruby-crowned Kinglet. Common transient throughout state; rare winter resident.

Subspecies in Kansas: *R. c. calendula* (Linnaeus).

Anthus spinoletta. Water Pipit. Common transient throughout state, more numerous in west.

Subspecies in Kansas: *A. s. rubescens* (Tunstall).

Anthus spragueii (Audubon). Sprague Pipit. Transient throughout state, perhaps more common in central or western parts; status poorly known. Specimens known from Trego, Cloud, Greenwood, Woodson, and Anderson counties.

No subspecies recognized.

Bombycilla garrulus. Bohemian Waxwing. Rare winter visitant throughout state. Few specimens on record, from Riley, Shawnee, Jefferson, Greenwood, and Sedgwick counties.

Subspecies in Kansas: *B. g. pallidiceps* Reichenow.

* *Bombycilla cedrorum* Vieillot. Cedar Waxwing. Common transient and irregular winter resident throughout state; rare summer resident in northeast. Breeding records: four nests found at Lake Quivira, Wyandotte County, July 22, 1947 (nestling collected, KU 32374), July 3, 1949 (young in nest), July 4, 1950, July 10, 1952 (young in nest), Harold C. Hedges; nest found in Topeka, Shawnee County, June 16, 1953, Cliff Olander and T. W. Nelson.

No subspecies recognized.

Lanius excubitor. Northern Shrike. Winter resident, rare in east, uncommon in west.

Subspecies in Kansas: *L. e. borealis* Vieillot in east, *L. e. invictus* Grinnell in west (most specimens from Kansas are intermediate between the two).

* *Lanius ludovicianus.* Loggerhead Shrike. Common resident and transient throughout state, but may leave north-central and northwestern parts in winter.

Subspecies in Kansas: *L. l. migrans* Palmer in extreme east, *L. l. excubitorides*

Swainson in west, east to Norton, Ness, and Clark counties; birds from rest of state mostly intermediate.

* *Sturnus vulgaris.* Starling. Introduced. First appeared in early 1930's, now common transient and resident throughout state.

Subspecies in Kansas: *S. v. vulgaris* Linnaeus.

* *Vireo atricapillus* Woodhouse. Black-capped Vireo. Summer resident in Comanche and possibly other south-central counties. Status poorly known. Goss collected three pairs in southeastern Comanche County, May 7 to 18, 1885, and found a nest under construction on May 11, 1885. Sight records from Manhattan, Riley County, June 18, 1953, by Scott Searles, and Halstead, Harvey County, May 16, 1951, by Edna L. Ruth.

No subspecies recognized.

* *Vireo griseus.* White-eyed Vireo. Locally common transient and summer resident in east. Status poorly known. Nesting records from Doniphan County (Linsdale) and Kansas City region; specimens taken in summer from Douglas, Montgomery, and Labette counties.

Subspecies in Kansas: *V. g. noveboracensis* (Gmelin).

* *Vireo bellii.* Bell Vireo. Common summer resident throughout state.

Subspecies in Kansas: *V. b. bellii* Audubon.

* *Vireo flavifrons* Vieillot. Yellow-throated Vireo. Uncommon transient and local, uncommon summer resident throughout state. Goss reported two nests, one with 1 Cowbird and 3 vireo eggs, at Neosho Falls, Woodson County, May 9, 1877, and one under construction at Topeka, Shawnee County, May 18, 1883. T. W. Nelson found a nest at Topeka in 1947 (date approximate). R. F. Miller found an occupied nest 3 miles north of Baldwin, Douglas County, May 6, 1947.

No subspecies recognized.

Vireo solitarius. Solitary Vireo. Fairly common transient throughout state.

Subspecies in Kansas: *V. s. solitarius* (Wilson) in east, *V. s. plumbeus* Coues and *V. s. cassinii* Xantus in west.

* *Vireo olivaceus* (Linnaeus). Red-eyed Vireo. Common transient and summer resident throughout state.

No subspecies recognized.

Vireo philadelphicus (Cassin). Philadelphia Vireo. Uncommon transient in east (often overlooked); reported west to Harvey County but western limit of migration in Kansas not known.

No subspecies recognized.

* *Vireo gilvus.* Warbling Vireo. Common transient and summer resident throughout state.

Subspecies in Kansas: *V. g. gilvus* (Vieillot).

* *Mniotilta varia* (Linnaeus). Black and White Warbler. Common transient throughout state, local and uncommon summer resident in east. Breeding distribution in state poorly known. Nests reported in Douglas and Leavenworth counties.

No subspecies recognized.

* *Protonotaria citrea* (Boddaert). Prothonotary Warbler. Locally common transient and summer resident in eastern Kansas. Nesting records from Doniphan, Leavenworth, Johnson, Douglas, Shawnee, and Woodson counties.

No subspecies recognized.

* *Helmitheros vermivorus* (Gmelin). Worm-eating Warbler. Rare transient (specimens from Doniphan, Douglas, and Woodson counties) and summer resident in east. Linsdale saw a singing bird on July 11, 1923, in Doniphan County. Hilton (Wilson Bull., 32, 1920:85-86) reports finding a newly-fledged young bird with an adult at Fort Leavenworth, Leavenworth County, on June 7, 1919 (some of Hilton's records seem highly improbable, but the one in question is convincing to me).

No subspecies recognized.

Vermivora chrysoptera (Linnaeus). Golden-winged Warbler. Rare transient in east. Several sight records and one specimen: female (KU 12700), 3 miles south of Lawrence, Douglas County, May 2, 1921, E. R. Hall.

No subspecies recognized.

Vermivora pinus (Linnaeus). Blue-winged Warbler. Uncommon transient in east. Possibly nests rarely but no definite evidence.

No subspecies recognized.

Vermivora peregrina (Wilson). Tennessee Warbler. Common transient in east, uncommon transient in west.

No subspecies recognized.

Vermivora celata. Orange-crowned Warbler. Common transient throughout state.

Subspecies in Kansas: *V. c. celata* (Say) throughout state, *V. c. orestera* Oberholser in west.

Vermivora ruficapilla. Nashville Warbler. Common transient throughout state.

Subspecies in Kansas: *V. r. ruficapilla* (Wilson).

Vermivora virginiae (Baird). Virginia Warbler. Transient in extreme west. Known in Kansas only from 8 miles south of Richfield, Morton County: five birds seen, two collected, May 4 to 10, 1950, Richard and Jean Graber.

No subspecies recognized.

* *Parula americana* (Linnaeus). Parula Warbler. Fairly common transient and local summer resident in eastern Kansas. Nesting records from Riley, Doniphan, Douglas, and Woodson counties; western limit of breeding distribution unknown.

No subspecies recognized.

* *Dendroica petechia.* Yellow Warbler. Common transient and summer resident throughout state.

Subspecies in Kansas: *D. p. aestiva* (Gmelin) breeding in all except southwestern Kansas; *D. p. sonorana* Brewster probably breeding in extreme southwest (specimens from Morton County); *D. p. rubiginosa* (Pallas) transient, probably throughout state.

Dendroica magnolia (Wilson). Magnolia Warbler. Uncommon transient throughout state.

No subspecies recognized.

Dendroica tigrina (Gmelin). Cape May Warbler. Rare transient in east. Several sight records but only one specimen from state: immature male (KU 31644), Lawrence, Douglas County, December 6, 1954 (abnormally late date), Mary Edith Kizer.

No subspecies recognized.

Dendroica caerulescens. Black-throated Blue Warbler. Rare transient, more records from west than from east.

Subspecies in Kansas: *D. c. caerulescens* (Gmelin).

Dendroica coronata. Myrtle Warbler. Common transient throughout state, rare winter resident. (See also Audubon Warbler.)

Subspecies in Kansas: *D. c. coronata* (Linnaeus) and *D. c. hooveri* McGregor.

Dendroica auduboni. Audubon Warbler. Common transient in west, rare in east, specimens taken east to Trego County. Hybrids between this species and Myrtle Warbler common in west.

Subspecies in Kansas: *D. a. auduboni* (Townsend).

Dendroica nigrescens (Townsend). Black-throated Gray Warbler. Common transient in extreme western Kansas. Several sight records and four specimens from 8 miles south of Richfield, Morton County, May 8 to 13, 1950, Richard and Jean Graber.

No subspecies recognized.

Dendroica townsendi (Townsend). Townsend Warbler. Transient in extreme western Kansas. Five records: all from 8 miles south of Richfield, Morton County, May 3 (female collected), 11, and 20, 1950, September 3 and 5 (immature female, KU 31206), 1952, Richard and Jean Graber.

No subspecies recognized.

Dendroica virens. Black-throated Green Warbler. Transient, uncommon in east and rare in west.

Subspecies in Kansas: *D. v. virens* (Gmelin).

Dendroica cerulea (Wilson). Cerulean Warbler. Uncommon transient and possibly summer resident in east, but status poorly known. No definite nesting record. Only five specimens on record.

No subspecies recognized.

Dendroica fusca (Müller). Blackburnian Warbler. Transient, uncommon in east, rare in west.

No subspecies recognized.

[*Dendroica dominica.* Sycamore Warbler. A few sight records from east and possibly breeds in southeast but placed on Hypothetical List until a specimen from state is obtained.]

Dendroica pensylvanica (Linnaeus). Chestnut-sided Warbler. Transient, fairly common in east, uncommon in west. Only three specimens from state, two from Shawnee County, one from Morton County.

No subspecies recognized.

Dendroica castanea (Wilson). Bay-breasted Warbler. Uncommon transient throughout state.

No subspecies recognized.

Dendroica striata (Forster). Black-poll Warbler. Common transient in east, uncommon or rare in west.

No subspecies recognized.

[*Dendroica pinus.* Pine Warbler. Probably rare transient in east where several have been reported seen, but placed in Hypothetical List in absence of a specimen from Kansas. Linsdale reported taking a Pine Warbler in Doniphan County, September 13, 1923, but the specimen is actually a Cerulean Warbler.]

* *Dendroica discolor.* Prairie Warbler. Known to occur regularly only in Wyandotte and Johnson counties, where locally common transient and summer resident; newly fledged young have been found. One specimen: male (KU 32376), 2 miles west of Lake Quivira, Johnson County, May 3, 1942, Harold C. Hedges.

Subspecies in Kansas: *D. d. discolor* (Vieillot).

Dendroica palmarum. Palm Warbler. Uncommon transient in east, west at least to Cloud County. Western limit of occurrence in migration not known.

Subspecies in Kansas: *D. p. palmarum* (Gmelin).

* *Seiurus aurocapillus.* Oven-bird. Fairly common transient throughout state; local summer resident in northeast. Brumwell reported one pair nesting in June, 1939, and in 1940, at Fort Leavenworth, Leavenworth County. His report is lacking in details but no other nesting records are available.

Subspecies in Kansas: *S. a. aurocapillus* (Linnaeus) throughout state, *S. a. cinereus* A. H. Miller taken in Cheyenne County.

Seiurus noveboracensis. Northern Water-thrush. Fairly common transient throughout state.

Subspecies in Kansas: *S. n. notabilis* Ridgway.

* *Seiurus motacilla* (Vieillot). Louisiana Water-thrush. Fairly common transient and summer resident in east, uncommon transient in west. Approximately 11 breeding records, all from Miami and Linn counties. Summer distribution in state inadequately known.

No subspecies recognized.

* *Oporornis formosus* (Wilson). Kentucky Warbler. Common transient and summer resident in east. Nests west to Riley County, but not reported from Cloud County by Porter.

No subspecies recognized.

Oporornis philadelphia (Wilson). Mourning Warbler. Locally common transient in east, west rarely to Sedgwick and Cloud counties. Sight records supposedly of Connecticut Warblers (*Oporornis agilis*) may, at least in part, refer to this species. No specimens of *O. agilis* known from state.

No subspecies recognized.

Oporornis tolmiei. Macgillivray Warbler. Common transient in extreme western Kansas, accidental in east. Specimens from Morton, Hamilton, and Marshall (1) counties.

Subspecies in Kansas: *O. t. monticola* Phillips.

* *Geothlypis trichas.* Yellow-throat. Common transient throughout state; common summer resident in east, less common in west.

Subspecies in Kansas: *G. t. brachidactyla* (Swainson) breeds in east; *G. t. occidentalis* Brewster breeds in west. Distribution in Kansas of these subspecies and identity of transients poorly known.

* *Icteria virens.* Yellow-breasted Chat. Common transient and summer resident, perhaps less common in west.

Subspecies in Kansas: *I. v. virens* (Linnaeus) in east, *I. v. auricollis* (Lichtenstein) in west, intergrading through most of state.

Wilsonia citrina (Boddaert). Hooded Warbler. Formerly common summer resident in east, now rare and perhaps no longer nests in state. No satisfactory breeding record. Three males from Leavenworth County, May 9, 1871, and one from Shawnee County, May 17, 1871, taken by J. A. Allen, are now at Harvard.

No subspecies recognized.

Wilsonia pusilla. Wilson Warbler. Common transient throughout state.

Subspecies in Kansas: *W. p. pusilla* (Wilson) in east, *W. p. pileolata* (Pallas) in west; precise distribution in migration unknown.

Wilsonia canadensis (Linnaeus). Canada Warbler. Uncommon transient in east, reported west to Sedgwick and Cloud counties.

No subspecies recognized.

* *Setophaga ruticilla.* American Redstart. Common transient and local summer resident in east; probably only transient in west but breeding range in state poorly known. Few definite nesting records: Brumwell reported nesting at Fort Leavenworth, Leavenworth County; J. M. Porter found a nest in Republic County, May 22, 1940.

Subspecies in Kansas: *S. r. ruticilla* (Linnaeus) is breeding form; *S. r. tricolora* (Müller) occurs in migration.

* *Passer domesticus.* English Sparrow. Introduced. Common resident throughout state.

Subspecies in Kansas: *P. d. domesticus* (Linnaeus).

* *Dolichonyx oryzivorus* (Linnaeus). Bobolink. Transient, uncommon in east and rare in west in spring; rare in east and absent in west in fall. In 1940, several pairs remained until July 21 near Jamestown State Lake, Cloud County, and two pairs were seen feeding fledglings on June 25 (J. M. Porter). No other good evidence of breeding.

No subspecies recognized.

* *Sturnella magna.* Eastern Meadowlark. Common transient and resident in eastern part. Nests locally west to Jewell County in north and Barber County in south. Less common in winter.

Subspecies in Kansas: *S. m. magna* (Linnaeus) in northeast, *S. m. argutula* Bangs in southeast.

Sturnella neglecta. Western Meadowlark. Common transient and resident in western part. Nests commonly east to Flint Hills, irregularly and uncommonly in east. Largely replaces Eastern Meadowlark in east in winter.

Subspecies in Kansas: *S. n. neglecta* Audubon.

* *Xanthocephalus xanthocephalus* (Bonaparte). Yellow-headed Blackbird. Transient, common in west and uncommon in east, and uncommon, local summer resident. Breeds more frequently in west; nesting records from Meade, Wallace, Barton, Stafford, Doniphan, and Douglas counties. One winter record, Riley County.

No subspecies recognized.

* *Agelaius phoeniceus.* Red-wing. Common transient and summer resident throughout state, less common winter resident.

Subspecies in Kansas: *A. p. phoeniceus* (Linnaeus) breeds in most of state; *A. p. fortis* Ridgway may nest in west and occurs in migration; *A. p. arctolegus* Oberholser occurs in migration.

* *Icterus spurius* (Linnaeus). Orchard Oriole. Common transient and summer resident throughout state.

No subspecies recognized.

Icterus cucullatus. Hooded Oriole. Accidental. One record: bird banded at Los Angeles, California, January 22, 1939, found dead by Dr. F. S. Williams, 16 miles southeast of Garden City, Finney County, about August 5, 1939; foot of specimen preserved.

Subspecies in Kansas: *I. c. californicus* (Lesson), on geographic grounds.

* *Icterus galbula* (Linnaeus). Baltimore Oriole. Common transient and summer resident through most of state; hybridizes freely with Bullock Oriole in west. One winter record: immature male (KU 31988), Lawrence, Douglas County, December 25, 1953, H. B. Tordoff.

No subspecies recognized.

* *Icterus bullockii.* Bullock Oriole. Common transient and summer resident in west, rarely east to Stafford County (breeding?) and Douglas County (transient).

Subspecies in Kansas: *I. b. bullockii* (Swainson).

Euphagus carolinus. Rusty Blackbird. Common transient and locally common winter resident throughout state.

Subspecies in Kansas: *E. c. carolinus* (Müller).

Euphagus cyanocephalus (Wagler). Brewer Blackbird. Transient and local winter resident. Common in west, uncommon in east. Probably nests in northwest, but no satisfactory evidence of this.

No subspecies recognized.

Quiscalus quiscula. Bronzed Grackle. Common transient and summer resident throughout state; local winter resident.

Subspecies in Kansas: *Q. q. versicolor* Vieillot.

* *Molothrus ater.* Cowbird. Common transient and summer resident throughout state; local winter resident.

Subspecies in Kansas: *M. a. ater* (Boddaert) is breeding bird; *M. a. artemisiae* Grinnell transient, common in west and possibly nesting in northwest.

Piranga ludoviciana (Wilson). Western Tanager. Fairly common transient and perhaps summer resident in extreme west. Two males taken 4½ miles west of Kendall, Hamilton County, May 20 and June 1, 1893, H. W. Menke; many seen and two males and a female (KU 31207) taken 8 miles south of Richfield, Morton County, May 6, 1950 (males) and September 4, 1952, Richard and Jean Graber.

No subspecies recognized.

* *Piranga olivacea* (Gmelin). Scarlet Tanager. Fairly common transient in east and uncommon summer resident in northeast. Distribution in state poorly known; breeding records from Doniphan, Leavenworth, and Cloud counties.

No subspecies recognized.

* *Piranga rubra.* Summer Tanager. Common transient and summer resident, distribution poorly known. Recorded in migration (possibly breeding?) west to Morton County and breeding in Doniphan and Douglas counties. Not reported by Porter as nesting in Cloud County.

Subspecies in Kansas: *P. r. rubra* (Linnaeus).

* *Richmondena cardinalis.* Cardinal. Common resident in east, uncommon in west, rare in extreme southwest.

Subspecies in Kansas: *R. c. cardinalis* (Linnaeus).

* *Pheucticus ludovicianus* (Linnaeus). Rose-breasted Grosbeak. Common transient and locally common summer resident in east. Reported in summer west to Rawlins County; probably absent in summer from southeast. Distribution poorly known.

No subspecies recognized.

* *Pheucticus melanocephalus.* Black-headed Grosbeak. Common transient and summer resident in west, nesting east to Cloud and Harvey counties. Occasionally occurs farther east in migration.

Subspecies in Kansas: *P. m. melanocephalus* (Swainson).

* *Guiraca caerulea.* Blue Grosbeak. Common transient and summer resident in most of state; locally common in summer in northeast.

Subspecies in Kansas: *G. c. caerulea* (Linnaeus) in east, *G. c. interfusa* Dwight and Griscom in west; most specimens from state are intergrades.

Passerina cyanea (Linnaeus). Indigo Bunting. Common transient and summer resident west to Finney County, status in extreme west not known but probably absent there.

No subspecies recognized.

Passerina amoena (Say). Lazuli Bunting. Common transient and probably summer resident in extreme western Kansas. No breeding record. Rare in east in migration.

No subspecies recognized.

* *Passerina ciris.* Painted Bunting. Fairly common summer resident in east, west to Barber and north to Riley and Shawnee counties. One positive nesting record: nest with young, successfully fledged, Lawrence, Douglas County, spring and summer, 1918, Bessie D. Reed.

Subspecies in Kansas: *P. c. pallidior* Mearns.

* *Spiza americana* (Gmelin). Dickcissel. Transient and summer resident throughout state; common in east, locally common in west.

No subspecies recognized.

Hesperiphona vespertina. Evening Grosbeak. Rare and irregular winter visitant. Reported from widely scattered localities throughout state.

Subspecies in Kansas: *H. v. vespertina* (Cooper); *H. v. brooksi* Grinnell may occur in west.

Carpodacus purpureus. Purple Finch. Fairly common transient and winter resident in east; status in west not known.

Subspecies in Kansas: *C. p. purpureus* (Gmelin).

Carpodacus mexicanus. House Finch. Occurs in southwestern Kansas, reported common north to Hamilton County and east to Finney County. One record from Concordia, Cloud County, 2 or 3 birds seen from February 26 to March 6, 1954, Lillie and Ida Cook, J. M. Porter. Most records in winter; status in summer uncertain.

Subspecies in Kansas: *C. m. frontalis* (Say).

[*Pinicola enucleator.* Pine Grosbeak. One old record (possibly based on a specimen, but convincing details are lacking) and a few recent sight records from east. Placed in Hypothetical List in absence of an authentic specimen from state.]

Acanthis flammea. Redpoll. Rare and irregular winter visitant. Records from Cloud, Riley (specimen), Douglas (specimens), and Woodson counties, and Kansas City region.

Subspecies in Kansas: *A. f. flammea* (Linnaeus).

* *Spinus pinus.* Pine Siskin. Common but irregular transient and winter resident throughout state. Two breeding records: nest with 3 or 4 young, later successfully fledged, Onaga, Pottawatomie County, May 3, 1920, F. F. Crevecoeur; nest with 3 eggs (young successfully fledged), 1 mile southwest of Concordia, Cloud County, observed from April 6 to 30, 1954, J. M. Porter.

Subspecies in Kansas: *S. p. pinus* (Wilson).

* *Spinus tristis.* Eastern Goldfinch. Common resident throughout state.

Subspecies in Kansas: *S. t. tristis* (Linnaeus).

* *Loxia curvirostra.* Red Crossbill. Irregular winter visitant throughout state, locally common at times. One nesting record: nest with one egg, Topeka, Shawnee County, March 22, 1917, A. Sidney Hyde. This nest later held three eggs, all hatched, three young fledged, and the family left the area in June.

Subspecies in Kansas (in approximate decreasing order of frequency): *L. c. benti* Griscom, *L. c. bendirei* Ridgway, *L. c. minor* (Brehm), *L. c. stricklandi* Ridgway, *L. c. sitkensis* Grinnell.

Loxia leucoptera. White-winged Crossbill. Rare and irregular winter visitant throughout the state. Only two specimens taken (Douglas and Ellis counties).

Subspecies in Kansas: *L. l. leucoptera* Gmelin.

Chlorura chlorura (Audubon). Green-tailed Towhee. Fairly common transient in west; rare winter visitant in east (Shawnee County, Wyandotte County).

No subspecies recognized.

* *Pipilo erythrophthalmus.* Red-eyed Towhee. Common transient and winter resident throughout state; uncommon summer resident in east, status in west in summer not known. No nest found, but recently fledged young reported in several counties.

Subspecies in Kansas: *P. e. erythrophthalmus* (Linnaeus) resident; *P. e. arcticus* (Swainson) winter resident throughout state; *P. e. montanus* Swarth reported as transient only from Morton County.

* *Calamospiza melanocorys* Stejneger. Lark Bunting. Common transient and summer resident in west, rare transient in east. Nesting in southwestern Kansas irregular; absent some years and present in other years. One nesting record from east, in Franklin County.

No subspecies recognized.

Passerculus sandwichensis. Savannah Sparrow. Common transient and rare winter resident throughout state.

Subspecies in Kansas: *P. s. savanna* (Wilson), *P. s. nevadensis* Grinnell, *P. s. oblitus* Peters and Griscom.

* *Ammodramus savannarum.* Grasshopper Sparrow. Common transient and local summer resident throughout state.

Subspecies in Kansas: *A. s. perpallidus* (Coues).

Ammodramus bairdii (Audubon). Baird Sparrow. One record: male? (U. S. Natl. Mus. 155884), Pendennis, Lane County, April 25, 1897, J. A. Loring. This species probably occurs regularly in the state but is overlooked.

No subspecies recognized.

Passerherbulus caudacutus (Latham). Leconte Sparrow. Common transient and irregular, locally common winter resident west at least to Lane County.

No subspecies recognized.

* *Passerherbulus henslowii.* Henslow Sparrow. Uncommon transient and uncommon, local summer resident in east, west at least to Cloud County. Breeding records from Morris, Shawnee, Douglas, and Anderson counties.

Subspecies in Kansas: *P. h. henslowii* (Audubon).

Ammospiza caudacuta. Sharp-tailed Sparrow. Rare transient in east. Specimens taken in Shawnee, Douglas, Woodson, and McPherson counties. Supposed nesting reported by Goss probably erroneous.

Subspecies in Kansas: *A. c. nelsoni* (Allen).

Pooecetes gramineus. Vesper Sparrow. Common transient throughout state. May nest in northwest but no evidence available.

Subspecies in Kansas: *P. g. gramineus* (Gmelin) in east, *P. g. confinis* Baird in west.

* *Chondestes grammacus.* Lark Sparrow. Common transient and summer resident throughout state.

Subspecies in Kansas: *C. g. grammacus* (Say) east of Flint Hills, *C. g. strigatus* Swainson in west; the two subspecies intergrade in central Kansas.

Aimophila ruficeps. Rufous-crowned Sparrow. Two records: male (KU 29222), Schwarz Canyon, Comanche County, June 7, 1936, C. W. Hibbard; one seen near Point Rock, Morton County, May 21, 1950, Richard and Jean Graber.

Subspecies in Kansas: *A. r. scottii* (Sennett).

Aimophila aestivalis. Pine-woods Sparrow. One specimen: male (KU 32377), Lake Quivira, in Wyandotte County, April 26, 1948, Harold C. Hedges. One seen, Lake Quivira, in Johnson County, April 24, 1949, Harold C. Hedges.

Subspecies in Kansas: *A. a. illinoensis* (Ridgway).

* *Aimophila cassinii* (Woodhouse). Cassin Sparrow. Common summer resident in southwestern Kansas, known north to Hamilton County and east to Finney County. One nesting record: nest with two young and one pipped egg, one mile south of Garden City, Finney County, May 24, 1954, Marvin D. Schwilling.

No subspecies recognized.

Amphispiza bilineata. Black-throated Sparrow. One record: specimen of unknown sex (KU 31356), 4 miles north and 3 miles east of Garden City, Finney County, November 25, 1952, Marvin D. Schwilling.

Subspecies in Kansas: *A. b. deserticola* Ridgway.

Junco aikeni Ridgway. White-winged Junco. Fairly common transient and winter resident in western Kansas. Specimens from Wallace, Ellis, Hamilton, and Morton counties.

No subspecies recognized.

Junco hyemalis. Slate-colored Junco. Common transient and winter resident throughout state.

Subspecies in Kansas: *J. h. hyemalis* (Linnaeus), *J. h. cismontanus* Dwight.

Junco oreganus. Oregon Junco. Common transient and winter resident in west, uncommon in east.

Subspecies in Kansas: *J. o. montanus* Ridgway, *J. o. mearnsi* Ridgway.

Spizella arborea. Tree Sparrow. Common transient and winter resident throughout state.

Subspecies in Kansas: *S. a. arborea* (Wilson) common in east; *S. a. ochracea* Brewster common throughout state.

* *Spizella passerina.* Chipping Sparrow. Common transient and summer resident in east, less common in west. Only two actual nesting records: occupied nest at Lawrence, Douglas County, May, 1954, James S. Findley; nest with 4 large young, 6 miles south of Atchison, Atchison County, May, 1934 or 1935, Homer A. Stephens (photographs taken of nest and adult).

Subspecies in Kansas: *S. p. passerina* (Bechstein) in east, *S. p. arizonae* Coues in west.

Spizella pallida (Swainson). Clay-colored Sparrow. Common transient throughout state. Possibly breeds in northwest: male (KU 31950) with greatly enlarged testes (9 × 6 mm.), 1 mile north of St. Francis, Cheyenne County, June 12, 1954, H. B. Tordoff.

No subspecies recognized.

Spizella breweri. Brewer Sparrow. Common transient in west. Five specimens known: four males, Morton County, April 8 to May 1, 1950, Richard and Jean Graber; one specimen (sex?), Finney County, May 3, 1954, Marvin D. Schwilling.

Subspecies in Kansas: *S. b. breweri* Cassin.

* *Spizella pusilla.* Field Sparrow. Common transient and summer resident and uncommon winter resident throughout state.

Subspecies in Kansas: *S. p. arenacea* Chadbourne, intergrading in east with *S. p. pusilla* (Wilson).

Zonotrichia querula (Nuttall). Harris Sparrow. Common transient and winter resident in east, uncommon in west.

No subspecies recognized.

Zonotrichia leucophrys. White-crowned Sparrow. Common transient and winter resident throughout state.

Subspecies in Kansas: *Z. l. leucophrys* (Forster) common in east, uncommon in west; *Z. l. gambelii* (Nuttall) common in west, fairly common in east.

Zonotrichia albicollis (Gmelin). White-throated Sparrow. Fairly common transient, uncommon winter resident west at least to Cloud and Sedgwick counties. Status in west poorly known; not reported at Garden City by Marvin D. Schwilling.

No subspecies recognized.

Passerella iliaca. Fox Sparrow. Fairly common transient and uncommon winter resident in east; probably occurs in west but status there poorly known.

Subspecies in Kansas: *P. i. iliaca* (Merrem); other subspecies may be found in west when specimens become available.

Melospiza lincolnii. Lincoln Sparrow. Common transient and uncommon winter resident throughout state.

Subspecies in Kansas: *M. l. lincolnii* (Audubon) throughout state; *M. l. alticola* (Miller and McCabe) in extreme west.

Melospiza georgiana. Swamp Sparrow. Common transient and uncommon winter resident in east. Western limit of range in Kansas not known (rare transient in Cloud and Finney counties—Porter and Schwilling).

Subspecies in Kansas: *M. g. georgiana* (Latham), *M. g. ericrypta* Oberholser.

Melospiza melodia. Song Sparrow. Common transient and winter resident throughout state.

Subspecies in Kansas: *M. m. euphonia* Wetmore, *M. m. juddi* Bishop, *M. m. montana* Henshaw.

Rhynchophanes mccownii (Lawrence). McCown Longspur. Transient, common in west, rare in east, and winter resident, uncommon in west, rare in east.

No subspecies recognized.

Calcarius lapponicus. Lapland Longspur. Common transient and winter resident throughout state.

Subspecies in Kansas: *C. l. lapponicus* (Linnaeus) is the common form; *C. l. alascensis* Ridgway occurs uncommonly (specimens from Douglas and Hamilton counties).

Calcarius pictus (Swainson). Smith Longspur. Fairly common transient and locally common winter resident except in extreme east, where rare.

No subspecies recognized.

* *Calcarius ornatus* (Townsend). Chestnut-collared Longspur. Common transient and winter resident in west, uncommon in east. Formerly, at least, occurred in summer in High Plains of west; nests found in Ellis County in 1871 by J. A. Allen. No recent records in summer.

No subspecies recognized.

Plectrophenax nivalis. Snow Bunting. Winter visitant at irregular and, sometimes, long intervals. No specimens preserved in state since 1879.

Subspecies in Kansas: *P. n. nivalis* (Linnaeus).

Transmitted May 19, 1955.

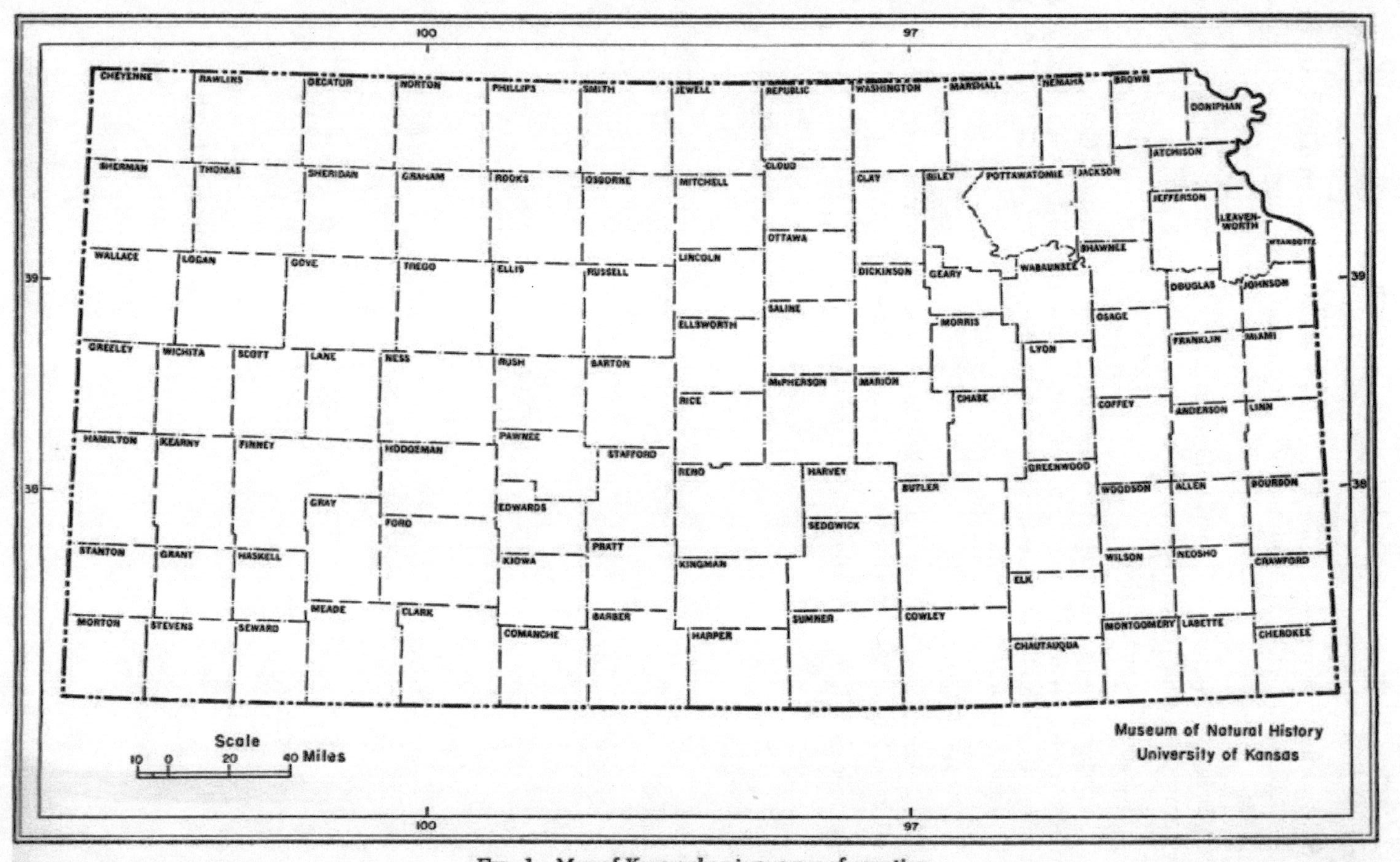

FIG. 1. Map of Kansas showing names of counties.

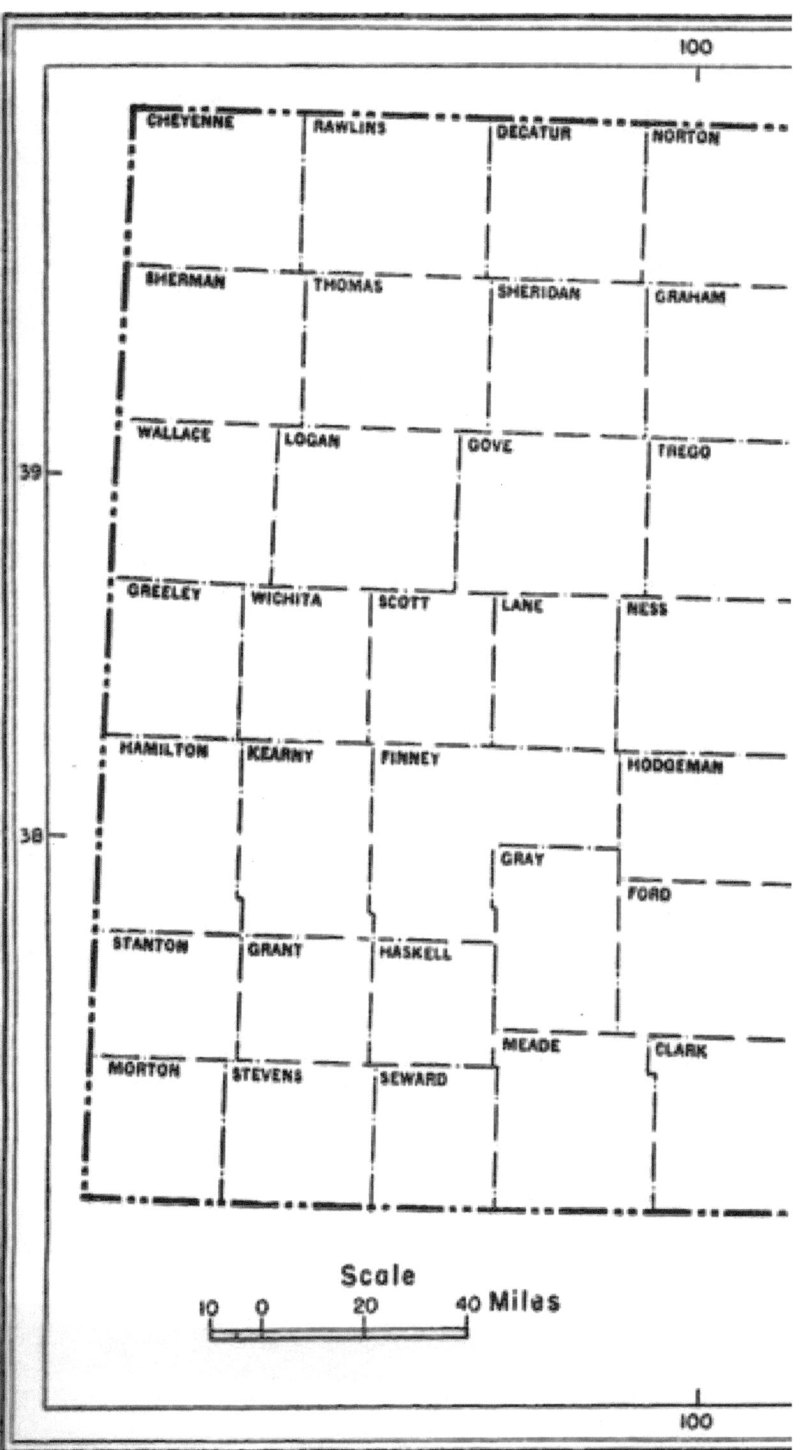

100
CHEYENNE
RAWLINS
DECATUR
NORTON
SHERMAN
THOMAS
SHERIDAN
GRAHAM
WALLACE
LOGAN
GOVE
TREGO
39
GREELEY
WICHITA
SCOTT
LANE
NESS
HAMILTON
KEARNY
FINNEY
HODGEMAN
38
GRAY
FORD
STANTON
GRANT
HASKELL
MEADE
CLARK
MORTON
STEVENS
SEWARD
Scale
10   0   20   40 Miles
100

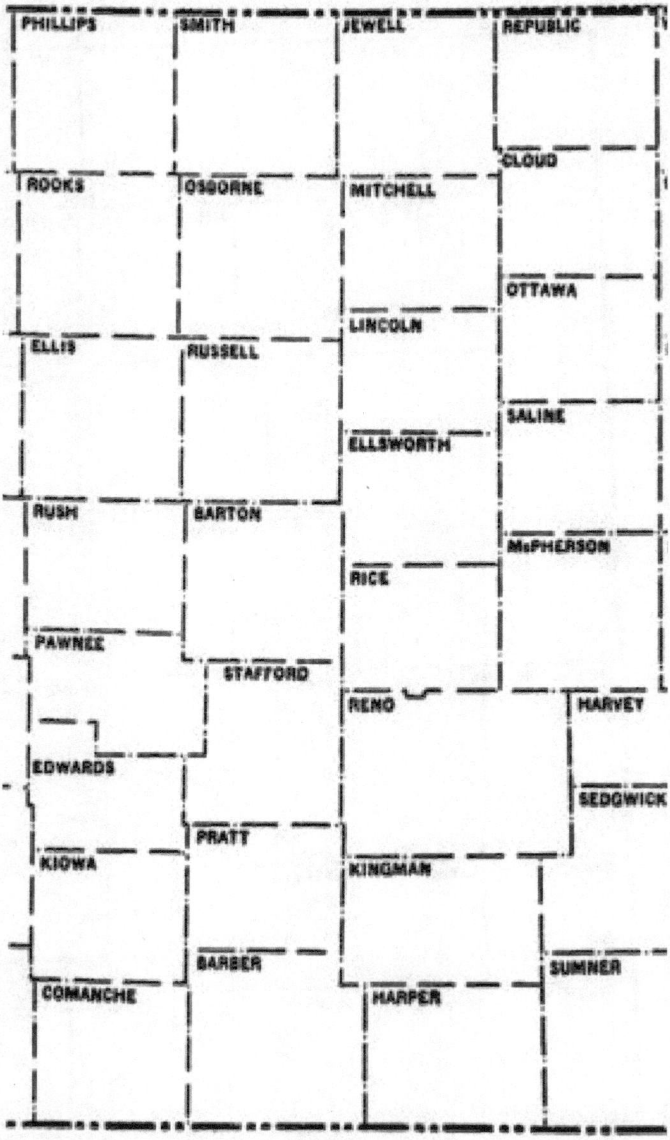

PHILLIPS
SMITH
JEWELL
REPUBLIC
ROOKS
OSBORNE
MITCHELL
CLOUD
OTTAWA
ELLIS
RUSSELL
LINCOLN
SALINE
ELLSWORTH
RUSH
BARTON
McPHERSON
RICE
PAWNEE
STAFFORD
RENO
HARVEY
EDWARDS
SEDGWICK
PRATT
KIOWA
KINGMAN
BARBER
SUMNER
COMANCHE
HARPER

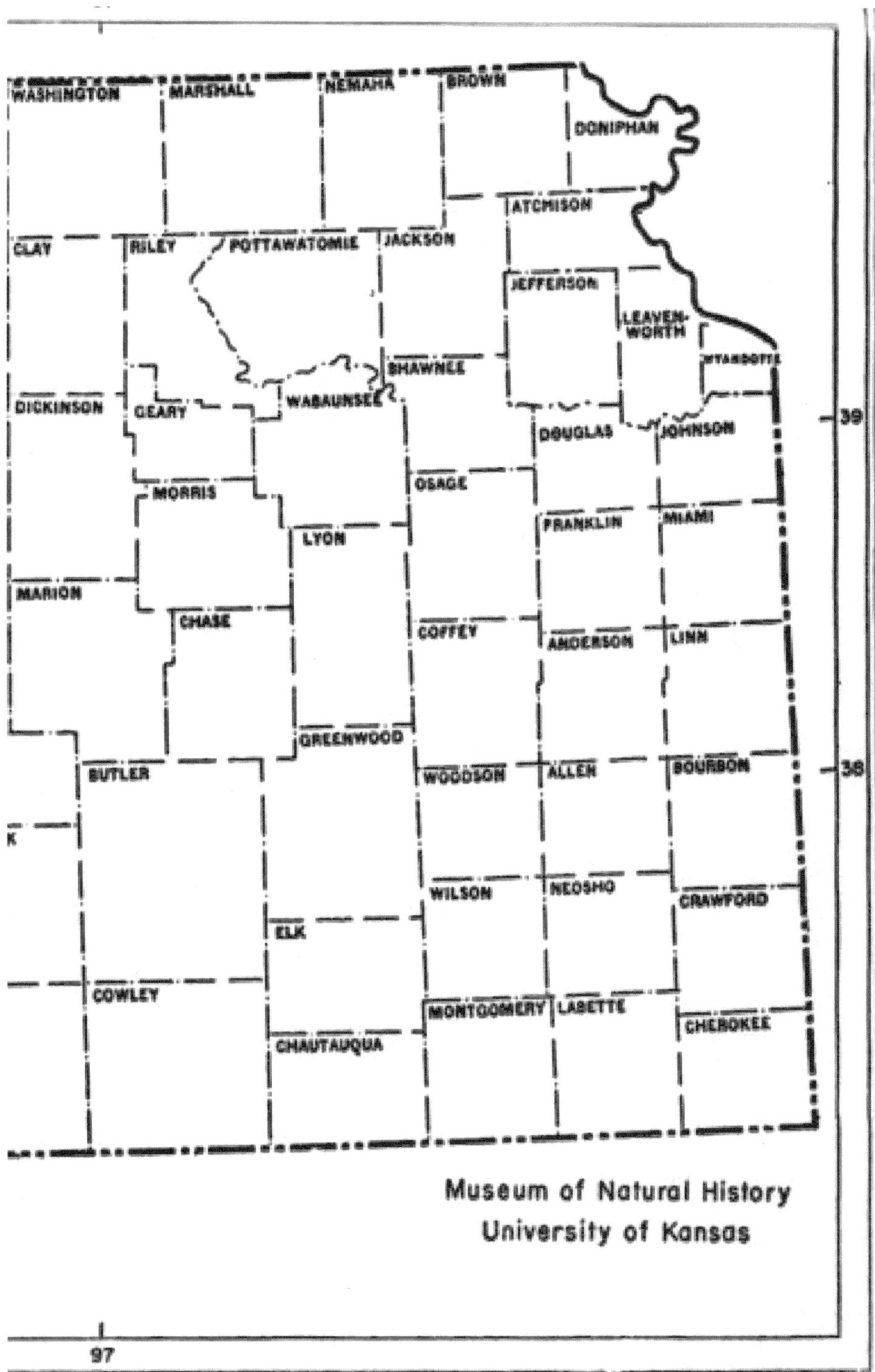

WASHINGTON
MARSHALL
NEMAHA
BROWN
DONIPHAN
ATCHISON
CLAY
RILEY
POTTAWATOMIE
JACKSON
JEFFERSON
LEAVEN-WORTH
DICKINSON
GEARY
WABAUNSEE
SHAWNEE
DOUGLAS
JOHNSON
WYANDOTTE
MORRIS
OSAGE
LYON
FRANKLIN
MIAMI
MARION
CHASE
COFFEY
ANDERSON
LINN
GREENWOOD
BUTLER
WOODSON
ALLEN
BOURBON
K
WILSON
NEOSHO
CRAWFORD
ELK
COWLEY
MONTGOMERY
LABETTE
CHEROKEE
CHAUTAUQUA
39
38
97
Museum of Natural History
University of Kansas

INDEX

C

Horned Lark *25*
Horned Owl *20*
House Finch *39*
House Wren *27*
Hudsonian Curlew *15*
Hudsonian Godwit *17*

I

Inca Dove *19*
Indigo Bunting *38*

K

Kentucky Warbler *35*
Killdeer *14*
King Eider *8*
King Rail *12*
Kittiwake *18*

L

Ladder-backed Woodpecker *23*
Lapland Longspur *43*
Lark *40*
Laughing Gull *18*
Lazuli Bunting *38*
Least Bittern *4*
Least Flycatcher *24*
Least Sandpiper *16*
Least Tern *19*
Leconte Sparrow *40*
Lesser Prairie Chicken *11*
Lesser Scaup Duck *7*
Lesser Yellow-legs *15*
Lewis Woodpecker *23*
Lincoln Sparrow *42*
Little Blue Heron *3*
Loggerhead Shrike *30*
Long-billed Curlew *14*
Long-billed Dowitcher *16*
Long-billed Marsh Wren *28*
Long-eared Owl *21*
Long-tailed Jaeger *17*
Louisiana Heron *3*
Louisiana Water-thrush *35*

M

Y

Lector House believes that a society develops through a two-fold approach of continuous learning and adaptation, which is derived from the study of classic literary works spread across the historic timeline of literature records. Therefore, we aim at reviving, repairing and redeveloping all those inaccessible or damaged but historically as well as culturally important literature across subjects so that the future generations may have an opportunity to study and learn from past works to embark upon a journey of creating a better future.

This book is a result of an effort made by Lector House towards making a contribution to the preservation and repair of original ancient works which might hold historical significance to the approach of continuous learning across subjects.

HAPPY READING & LEARNING!

LECTOR HOUSE LLP
E-MAIL: lectorpublishing@gmail.com